Living the
LOIS LEGACY:
PASSING ON A LASTING FAITH TO YOUR GRANDCHILDREN

The author, Helen (Westra) Hosier, at age three.

FOCUS ON THE FAMILY®

Living the LOIS LEGACY:

PASSING ON A LASTING FAITH TO YOUR GRANDCHILDREN

Helen Kooiman Hosier

FOREWORD BY EVELYN CHRISTENSON

LIVING THE LOIS LEGACY

A Focus on the Family book published by
Tyndale House Publishers, Wheaton, Illinois

Library of Congress Cataloging-in-Publication Data

Hosier, Helen Kooiman.
    Living the Lois legacy : passing on a lasting faith to your grandchildren / written
by Helen Kooiman Hosier ; foreword by Evelyn Christenson.
        p. cm. — (Focus on the Family)
Includes bibliographical references.
    ISBN 1-58997-056-X
  1. Grandparents, Religious life. 2. Grandparenting—Religious aspects—Christianity.
I. Title. II. Focus on the Family presents.
    BV4528.5 .H67 2002
    248.8'45—dc21

                                                            2002005309

To honor the memories of godly grandparents who passed on to their grandchildren a legacy of faith; and to motivate and inspire today's grandparents to be faithful in doing the same.

In particular, to those grandparents who so lovingly gave of themselves to my children with their remarkable wisdom, patience, kindness, and virtue:

Grandma Hattie Brunsting Westra,
my beloved mother, maternal grandmother
Grandma Esther Van Steenwyk Kooiman,
paternal grandmother
Grandpa Peter John Kooiman, paternal grandfather

The memory of the righteous is blessed.
—PROVERBS 10:7a (NASB)

CONTENTS

FOREWORD

Here is one of the most important books for grandparents ever written. The generation that comprises today's grandparents seemingly was unappreciated following the rebellion of young people in the 1960s and 1970s. But amid the recent family upheavals in our country, these older Americans are playing a tremendous role by providing continuity, security, and belonging for the largest group of adolescents to come along since the baby boomers—the millennial generation, born from 1982 on.

If you are heartbroken over the recent moral decay and chaos in our country and even in your own family, here are ways you can make a profound difference. If you are a grandparent feeling no longer needed—or helpless to be an influence in a critical situation in your extended family—this book is for you.

Helen Hosier's riveting real-life stories bring an indisputable credibility to the wonderful lessons she gleans from them. No empty theories about what she thinks will work, but actual heart-warming, hope-giving road maps to guide grandparents in how to fill the current unnatural gap between generations. What to do. What not to do. When something must be done. When to step into the bureaucratic system. When not to. All these questions go to build a beautiful bridge across the generation gap.

Surprisingly, this generation gap is being spanned by the fastest-growing segment of the population in America today: the older adults. Grandmothers and grandfathers. Their mature wisdom, accrued by life's experiences, gives them insight, love, and understanding hearts as they frequently—and sacrificially—pick up where divorce, drugs, death, mental impairment, catastrophic illness, and terrorism leave children and teens shattered in their wake. Four million children under 18 years of age are actually being raised in grandparents' homes today.

Helen courageously tackles the family problems we usually try to keep secret, ignore, or just give up on because we have no idea how to handle them. She did massive research for many years, interviewing prominent and ordinary people to see how they handled these same problems. The power of this book is that they responded in their own words, unashamedly sharing their grief, fears, empathy, love, and victories. The result is a book brimming with instruction and encouragement for all of us. And through it all, Helen's deep love of her Savior and the sweet fragrance of her personality tenderly draw us ever closer to what God wants us to be.

But the ultimate credibility and power of this book lie in its solid biblical foundation. Beautiful, encouraging, motivating Scriptures abound in it. Every precept and lesson Helen skillfully teaches are not from a finite human mind but directly from God Himself through His recorded Word. And she reminds us how God has given each generation of grandparents the awesome privilege of communicating for Him His omniscient truths to the following generations.

A hug, a lap, a kind word, a touch, a smile, a story. Especially one about how much Jesus loves them. These are things grandparents are made of.

This book was named for one of the lesser-known grandmothers of history: Lois. Two books of the Bible are named for her grandson Timothy. Both his grandmother Lois and his mother, Eunice, taught him the Scriptures, making small Timothy wise unto salvation. But it was in Grandmother Lois that faith was first found in that family, giving to the apostle Paul the young man Timothy, his true child in the faith, and to us, two books of the Bible.

Although this book is primarily written for grandparents, even younger family members will discover treasures of wisdom in it for themselves.

Most of the respondents to Helen's research said the incredible influence their own godly grandparents had on them was by the lives they lived—by their example! And there was a consistent emphasis, she says, on the role played in the lives of faith-filled grandparents by prayer. How their grandchildren saw and listened to them pray had a tremendous impact in the lives of their hurting loved ones.

Helen's question from Jesus—"When the Son of Man comes, will He find faith on the earth?"—pierced my heart as I once again faced the horrifying reality that faith on planet Earth can be lost in one generation. The question Helen hauntingly reiterates is, will faith get passed on to the next generations? Faith that will make them ready also for their final trip, like the grandmother on one of the planes that hit the World Trade Center tower that horrible September 11, 2001?

Since faith can be lost in one generation, grandmothers and grandfathers hold a powerful key. So Helen, from the deep passion of her heart, focuses this book on passing on familial faith—

faith that can influence those closest to us for time and eternity. Grandparents are to be the defenders of the faith handed down to succeeding generations.

This book thrilled my heart with the incredible potential available to grandparents. It caused me to weep as I was reminded of my own children's deaths; it made me relive many of the fun times with our grandchildren; and it pained me at what I could have done but missed from being too busy. But most of all, it made me soberly evaluate myself when I read Helen's closing question: "How would you rate yourself as a Lois?"

How would you?

EVELYN CHRISTENSON

Evelyn Christenson, founder and president of United Prayer Ministry, is the author of more than a dozen books including *What Happens When Women Pray*. She and her husband, Chris, live in St. Paul, Minnesota.

ACKNOWLEDGMENTS

No book is ever the result of one person's efforts alone. In fact, someone has pointed out that even God used more than 40 writers to give us the Bible, His timeless masterpiece. And in His providence He gave to His children the responsibility and privilege of representing Him in all succeeding generations. I find it an awesome thought that God chooses to allow us to communicate for Him. When I came across Jesus' words asking, "When the Son of Man comes, will He find faith on the earth?" (Luke 18:8), my attention was arrested in such a way that I could not get away from the implication of His words. Thus my search began to find out how grandparents had been impacting the lives of grandchildren and passing on the baton of faith.

I gratefully acknowledge the many stories I received in response to a questionnaire that helped bring this book into being. Grandmas and grandpas love to talk about many aspects of being a grandparent, but specifically I wanted to focus on modeling familial faith. What did these grandparents do that helped kindle the fire of faith in their grandchildren's lives? What I got were stories that grandchildren, now many of them grandparents themselves, were able to recall as they reached back into their memory banks. They helped me gain a perspective on how previous generations took the admonitions of Old Testament passages to heart as they sought to do what God commanded. And through them, I saw how today's grandparents are providing consistent examples, modeling what it means to be one of God's children.

In the process of writing this book, I had an accident that set me aside for many months. It was the Stonebriar Community Church Marathon Fellowship, located in Frisco, Texas, who ministered to me through their prayers, meals, e-mails, cards, flowers, and visits. These people were an extension of the "everlasting arms," and I acknowledge with deepest gratitude what this meant to me.

"The eternal God is thy refuge, and underneath are the everlasting arms" (Deuteronomy 33:27, KJV). This verse was one of many scriptures that helped fortify and sustain me through two surgeries, and I thank Rev. Donner Atwood for reminding me of it. Karolyn Guentherman has been an "earth angel" in so many ways. Not only is she the personification of a true friend, but she is an exemplary grandmother as well. In particular, I acknowledge what the presence of Taylor and Jimmie Gardener, Wanda Sharpe, and Karolyn Guentherman did for me as I was wheeled into surgery. Lee and Lynn Hollahan and Lynn and Alice Guffee saw to it that I got to appointments. Each of the women in our WOW (Women of Worth) group blessed me in so many ways. Dr. Robert E. Mendonsa came to my rescue, and I owe a debt of gratitude to him. Thanks to each individual.

Dearest friends, both near and far, encouraged and blessed me with their prayers, letters, phone calls, and e-mails: Dr. and Mrs. Orrin Bowman, Phyllis Seminoff, Charles and Anna Karnopp, Vicki Bohe-Thackwell, Dick Ross, Gloria Hukle, the family of Larry and Marlene Lee, Earl and Mary Ann Mooney, Donna Skell, Ken and Carol Lancaster, Dan and Holli Lancaster, Ken and Kay Hull, Barbara Johnson, Bill and Ardyth Petersen,

Ed and Kim Hentschel, Paul and Marguerite Appling, Earl and
Alice Caudle, Les and Doris Sites, and Don and Eddie Huff.

Sincerest thanks to Mark Maddox, Jane Terry, and Michael
Silva at Focus on the Family for the warmth of your encouragement, which came through so clearly.

My dear children and grandchildren, and my sister-in-law,
Mary Kooiman, although far away, were sensitive to my needs.
And Kraig Kooiman, my son, how I thank God for you and the
way you took care of my every need in person. How blessed I am
to have such a supportive family!

All of these people prayed me through the writing of this
book. You are all "earth angels," and I love you dearly. Thank
you, simply said but deeply felt and meant.

1

KINDLING A FIRE OF FAITH

The righteous man walks in his integrity;
His children are blessed after him.
—PROVERBS 20:7 (NKJV)

Today, when one out of every two marriages is in danger of fail-
ing, and with so many Christian homes already fractured by
divorce, the structure of the family is in serious jeopardy. Are we
in danger of losing the legacy of faith handed down from previous generations to ours? This precious heritage, the values that
our grandparents, great-grandparents, and their predecessors
held so dear—what is going to happen to them?

Quite possibly each person reading this book would have to
admit that his or her life has been affected by the disintegration
of the family. It's not an exaggeration to say that it has become a
national epidemic.

When I turn on a TV or radio talk show, what I see and hear going on out there alarms and saddens me. In discussing the times in which we live with my friends and family, I find that for them the feeling is just as desperate. Charles Swindoll has said that savage times are upon us. Matthew 24:3-12 and 2 Timothy 3 speak clearly of the kinds of end-time conditions on planet Earth that we see all around us today. Jesus and Paul didn't pull any punches in telling it like it was going to be (and now is).

Can we as grandparents ignore these clear warnings and not prepare our grandchildren?

For instance, I was "blown out of the water" (as my grandchildren would say) when I listened to the conversation Bill O'Reilly had with Dan Rather on the Fox News Channel recently. This was well after the Lewinsky scandal, with Clinton out of office. O'Reilly asked Rather if he thought Bill Clinton was an honest man.

Rather responded, "Yes, I think he's an honest man."

O'Reilly was obviously shocked. "Do you, really?"

Rather was quick to reply. "I do."

Recovering from shock, but still finding this conversation incredible, O'Reilly asked, "Even though he lied to Jim Lehrer's face about the Lewinsky case?"

Rather's answer showed the extreme lengths many in the media will go to in rationalizing wrongdoing. "Who among us has not lied about something?"

O'Reilly: "Well, I didn't lie to anybody's face on national television. How can you say he's an honest guy?"

Rather: "Well, because I think he is. I think at core he's an honest person.… I think you can be an honest person and lie about a number of things."

To his credit, Bill O'Reilly shook his head and was clearly disturbed.

Rather's mentality is alive, well, and spouted on television, on the radio, and in the print media without letup. It's okay to lie; you can still call yourself an honest person. This is what our grandchildren are constantly told in one way or another. They can't be shielded from it; we live in a world gone wrong.

That is why our role as defenders of truth is cut out for us.

THE FAITH OF A LOIS

While I was writing this book, people would ask what I was working on. I would gladly tell them. Yet when I would offer the title, often I was met with blank stares. Not many were familiar with Paul's mention of Timothy's grandmother in 2 Timothy 1:5:

> *I have been reminded of your sincere faith, which first*
> *lived in your grandmother Lois and in your mother Eunice*
> *and, I am persuaded, now lives in you also.*

When that passage came to my attention, it struck me. I wondered *How?* How did she do it? How are others doing it today? And what constitutes a good handoff of the baton of faith?

These are the questions I posed to the many grandparents and grandchildren that make up this book. In the coming pages, you are going to read their responses: grandparents who modeled a lasting faith for their grandchildren. You will be encouraged and challenged, as I was, by these amazing stories of faith. The legacy *is* alive. My prayer is that as you read them, you will know that you can do the same for your grandchildren, and give them roots that will sustain them through the tumultuous times in which we now live.

Paul began his letter to Timothy by saying that he was thankful he was serving God with a pure conscience, "as my forefathers did" (2 Timothy 1:3). It was a comfort to him that he was of the seed of those who served God. To Paul, Christianity and Judaism were not the distinct religions we think of today: the former was an outgrowth of the latter. Christianity was Judaism's fulfillment, its culmination, its glory. The Jewishness of Christianity was plainly stated in Paul's expression of thanksgiving for the faith of his Jewish parents. That was the "unfeigned" or sincere faith he saw in Lois and Eunice, and that Timothy was now exercising.

Next, Paul expressed his joy as he thanked God that Timothy had also kept up the beliefs of his ancestors, but also that something more had been added to that faith. To be precise, *Someone* more. God in the flesh. The fulfillment of prophecy, born to a Jewish mother.

Lois is not mentioned again in the New Testament. That she passed on her faith to her daughter and grandson, and that they understood the Scriptures' promises, is all we know. We don't have the details surrounding her coming to know Christ. What we do know is that faith "first lived in her" and that this powerful force set the example for Timothy (and by consequence, us) to follow.

If Lois had not been faithful, would there even be two books in the Bible with her grandson's name? How important that faith was to the heart of her daughter Eunice and her grandson Timothy. And because she was faithful, Paul could write of this godly grandmother as he did and give us a glimpse of what caused Timothy to become the faith-filled man that he became.

It appears from the biblical account that Paul might have been something of a father figure to Timothy. Certainly, he was a spiritual mentor. We know nothing about Eunice's husband, the father of Timothy, except in Acts 16:1 where it is mentioned that he was Greek. We are led to believe that Timothy's familial faith was nurtured solely by his maternal grandmother and mother. Paul had put his hands on Timothy; that meant Timothy was a partner with him in ministering the gospel and sharing the teaching (2 Timothy 1:6).

Eunice and Lois must have rejoiced as they saw Paul's mantle fall, as it were, upon this much-loved young man. Never let anyone say that family religion is not of importance. That young man's faith was unspeakably precious. And never let anyone try to tell you that an inheritance of godly traditions cannot be passed on. Timothy had been brought up on God's Word.

But as for you, continue in what you have learned and have become convinced of, because you know those from whom you learned it, and how from infancy you have known the holy Scriptures, which are able to make you wise for salvation through faith in Christ Jesus.
(2 Timothy 3:14-15)

The commentator Matthew Henry says, in his rather quaint, Old English way, that it is a comfortable thing when children imitate the faith and holiness of their godly parents, and tread in their steps. He points to 3 John 4 where the beloved Apostle says, "I have no greater joy than to hear that my children are walking in the truth." Certainly those are words we grandparents would echo.

It's a strange but true fact that neither the Old Testament nor the New tells us that it is the responsibility of the church to be the primary teacher of the faith to the next generation. [The Bible] makes it clear that parents and grandparents are to be the prime channels of spiritual education.   —STEPHEN AND JANET BLY

DEFENDERS OF THE FAITH

In this society in which our grandchildren live, where the Bible is so viciously attacked and maligned, we are often the first and last line of defense for biblical truth. We need to be fortified, ready to give an answer to our grandchildren's questions. When we are called on to defend and explain to our grandchildren the veracity of the Scriptures, we should be able to do so with conviction and intelligence.

Paul continues in his letter: "All Scripture is God-breathed and is useful for teaching, rebuking, correcting and training in righteousness, so that the man of God may be thoroughly equipped for every good work" (2 Timothy 3:16-17). All Scripture is "God-breathed," inspired by God, and guided by the Holy Spirit (2 Peter 1:21). God superintended these human authors so that, even with their individual personalities, they could faithfully record God's message to man.

I remember only too well the long hours I was made to spend memorizing Bible verses and answers to catechism questions when I was a child. At one point, I thought life was nothing but memorization and giving up a big chunk of my time on Saturdays to go to catechism class. But there came a time in my life when those verses returned to rescue me from the pit of despair. To this day it is the teachings I learned as a child that provide the firm foundation on which my faith, my children's faith, and my grandchildren's faith now rest.

When I hear someone say, "I was born in a Christian home but..." and then they go on to speak disparagingly about their upbringing, something in me doesn't like that. For, sure, our parents might have made some mistakes, and sometimes well-meaning grandparents and relatives can shove religion down their children's throats. But "religion" is not where it's at. It's the *intent* of our parents' *hearts* that we need to recall. If the kind of training we received in our homes was *not* anti-Bible, anti-God, or anti-Christ, we would do better to remember the commandment which calls us to honor our fathers and mothers. This kind of respect, after all, is what we are trying to produce in our grandchildren.

Next, Paul talks about two troublemakers who had strayed

from the truth, "overthrow[ing] the faith of some," but then he says, "Nevertheless, the solid foundation of God stands...." (2 Timothy 2:18-19a, NKJV). Our grandchildren's friends, teachers in school, and others will say things to ridicule the Bible. But if our grandchildren have a firm foundation, their faith will remain firm and fixed. It can stand.

My father and mother didn't leave my brother, sister, and me much in the way of an earthly legacy—no vast real estate holdings, no stocks and bonds, no investments paying off handsomely; in fact, after he died, my father's savings and investments were wiped out in the Depression when the local bank was closed. What they did leave us is "an inheritance that can never perish, spoil or fade—kept in heaven...." (1 Peter 1:4).

I have been told that my father's dying words at age 34 were, "For me to live is Christ, and to die is gain," and that he laid his hands on my mother's tummy and pronounced a benediction on me, his unborn child.

It is true that we have to appropriate this faith for ourselves, just as an earthly legacy must be claimed to inherit what has been left. But that's what Timothy did, what I did, and what your grandchildren will do as well if you work to pass on this priceless legacy.

When Timothy left his home to become Paul's traveling companion and partner in ministry, he left with his own faith, not his grandmother's, not his mother's, and not Paul's. And that's what you and I as grandparents should seek to communicate to our grandchildren—that they, too, can have this special relationship with God.

LEADING THE WAY TO FAITH

Grandmother Lois and Mother Eunice are our predecessors in this matter of reproducing faith in our grandchildren. There are other mothers mentioned in the Bible, but these two New Testament women were special. They lived in a town called Lystra, located in what would be Turkey today. They likely attended synagogue services in a town some distance from where they lived, walking the dusty roads, riding their donkeys, weather no obstacle. We don't know exactly how this mother and daughter were introduced to the truth about Jesus, but many believe it was a result of hearing the apostle Paul and Barnabas (his traveling companion before Timothy) when they came to Lystra. They may have been believers before that, but we do know that as a result of Paul's teaching in Lystra, he and Barnabas made many disciples. It wasn't a very warm reception; in fact, they were stoned and dragged from the city.

Acts 14 is where we find the exciting narrative. I can't help speculating just a bit—were Lois, Eunice, and young Timothy among those who watched what happened to Paul? Could they have been there, helped get him back on his feet, maybe even nursed his wounds before he continued on his way? Is this how the apostle came to know them and witness their faith? Somehow, Paul survived that stoning and left the city with Barnabas, later returning to strengthen and encourage the disciples in the region to "remain true to the faith."

In Paul's letter to Timothy, in which he gives a charge to this young man, he reminds him of the sufferings, and the kinds of things that happened to him in Antioch, Iconium and Lystra, the persecutions he endured. Remember that Paul was in chains, writing from prison, yet he could say to young Timothy that the Lord rescued him from all of them:

> *...for which I am suffering even to the point of being chained like a criminal. But God's word is not chained. Therefore I endure everything for the sake of the elect, that they too may obtain the salvation that is in Christ Jesus, with eternal glory.* (2 Timothy 2:9-10)

I pause here to remind myself as I am reminding you, that we do well when we unashamedly tell our grandchildren about the trials we have experienced. We do them no favor by shielding them from our experiences, how we have been thrust into trusting God time after time, and of His faithfulness in rescuing us. How better can they learn what faith is about than by hearing it from our lips and reading it in our letters? How has our faith been strengthened and encouraged because of our trust and reliance on God in what we have been through?

I speak from many such experiences. Our grandchildren know what it means to pray for Grandpa and Grandma who are going through difficulties. They know, too, what it means for their grandparents to praise and thank God for answering prayer. Many times, prayers the grandchildren prayed have been specifically answered.

I love to recount for Dustin, my daughter Rhonda's son, how he, as a little guy of four, folded his hands and prayed so hard his knuckles were white, when they visited us in Fort Worth, Texas. "Dear God, please sell Grandpa and Grandma's house so they can move back to California and we can see them…" Shortly after that, I remind Dustin, our house sold and for six years we lived near enough to them that we saw them often.

He saw how God answered his prayer and he knows the importance of being faithful to God. In more recent times, he called to ask for prayer because he had the flu and wanted to go to church camp. Would he have asked for that if he hadn't known that God hears and answers prayer? (This is the same grandson I talk about in chapter 15 who endured and came through osteogenic sarcoma treatments for a year. Talk about answered prayer!)

Charles Swindoll points out that there is nothing more encouraging or more motivating than a model to keep us going; that by following the model of those who have gone before us, we can do more than survive. We can overcome. That is what is so needed by today's children: a model to follow.

The apostle Paul offered this prayer for the Christians in Ephesus. It is a good one for us to pray for our grandchildren.

…I kneel before the Father, from whom his whole family in heaven and on earth derives its name, [and] pray that out of his glorious riches he may strengthen you with power through his Spirit in your inner being, so that Christ may dwell in your hearts through faith. And I pray that you, being rooted and established in love, may have power,

together with all the saints, to grasp how wide and long and high and deep is the love of Christ, and to know this love that surpasses knowledge—that you may be filled to the measure of all the fullness of God. (Ephesians 3:14-19)

2

WALKING IN
THE FAITH

The silver-haired head is a crown of glory,
If it is found in the way of righteousness.
—PROVERBS 16:31 (NKJV)

For many years, my husband and I had the privilege of participating in a ministry to seniors in different parts of America. In
these churches, we observed a trend toward the graying of the
folks in the pews. Often, as I would glance around, I wondered,
Where are the younger families? Is faith being passed on?

Then one day, reading Luke's gospel, I came across Jesus'
words asking, "When the Son of Man comes, will He find faith
on the earth?" (Luke 18:8), and my attention was arrested. I could
not get away from the implications of those words: Faith can be
lost in one generation. Reading that verse, and coupling it with
my observations in so many churches around the country, I

launched into an all-out search to find out how grandparents are impacting the lives of their grandchildren for the faith.

As believing grandparents, our most important task is to communicate our faith in Christ to our grandchildren.

—JERRY AND JACK SCHREUR

"MY GRANDMA BROUGHT ME"

One Father's Day, in church, a little boy inadvertently supplied the answer to my question—at least the answer for that particular inner-city church where there was a significant number of older people. The pastor invited the children to the front for a special sermonette. As he sat on a stool with the children gathered around him, he asked them what day it was. "Father's Day!" they all chimed in. Then he asked them to describe their fathers.

One precocious child piped up. "Well, right now my father is at home sleeping. My grandma brought me." He pointed, and I heard a grandma groan in back of me.

Another darling little girl took her cue. "My daddy is at home reading the paper."

The thought occurred to me that Timothy might have identified with that young one.

"My dad likes to play ball with me," one neatly dressed little boy said.

"My daddy reads Bible stories."

"He rents videos for us to watch."

"Fathers pray," one wise young one responded. "My daddy is over there," he added and pointed to his justifiably proud father. The father smiled, and so did many in the congregation.

Yet as I sat there, I watched two little children, obviously brother and sister. He was playing with her hair, and she was holding tightly to him. Neither was well dressed. They looked sad, their eyes downcast. I observed other children who didn't respond either. I sensed that some of these children didn't have fathers living at home. I nearly broke down sobbing, and I couldn't take my eyes off this beautiful little brother and sister. The need for a book about the role of grandparents walking in the faith was born in my heart at that moment.

In actuality, most of the children in that congregation were from the neighborhood and came to the services without parents. As we drove up on Sundays, we would see them leaving their homes alone. It was also obvious that many of these darling little ones were getting themselves ready in the morning. They had discovered Vacation Bible School in the summer, and someone had kept in touch with them, so now they attended church and their own Sunday morning service. It was a tremendous ministry to this inner-city neighborhood, and as a result, a lot of surrogate grandparenting was generated in that church. It was so heartwarming after the church service to see the older members of the church looking for favorite little ones, who would also be looking for them. There was a lot of hugging and kissing going on. It would have melted your heart to see it.

How many of these dear little ones had been brought by grandmothers like the one I heard groan? And how many other grandparents were stifling groans, sighing inwardly, some of them with grandchildren in other states wondering about them that Father's Day?

THE LAW OF LOVE

Two questions I asked grandparents in a questionnaire I sent out were these: What are you doing to enhance the quality of your grandchildren's lives? and What are you doing to secure a relationship with your grandchildren that makes it possible for you to model faith?

Responses indicated that many grandparents are greatly concerned because their children are *not* passing on the values by which they were raised. Nurturing faith in their children is not a priority in many families where one or even both of the parents were raised in a family where the Bible was read, prayers were offered, and church attendance was a must. I sensed an undercurrent of sadness in some of my respondents' letters. And guilt. As one grandmother said, "Guilt with a capital *G.*"

On the other hand, there are adult children, now parents, in whose hearts the fire of faith *was* kindled and who are making known God's faithfulness and biblical truths to their children. These adults responded joyfully, relating what a tremendous influence their grandparents had on their lives.

In Isaiah 38:19, The Old Testament prophet Isaiah wrote that a father is to make known to his children God's faithfulness and truth. But that doesn't always happen, as more than one person responded. "My father didn't become a Christian until late in life," wrote one woman, "but my childhood and youth activities were always church-centered as a result of my grandparents' influence." An incredible number wrote something similar. The grandparents were just ordinary people, but theirs was an uncommon and influential faith.

This same woman, now a grandmother herself, went on to explain that her own two children were dedicated to the Lord as infants, that she and her husband read Bible stories to them and helped them participate in Sunday school, and that they attended church as a family.

And always at Christmas and Easter we emphasized the Christian significance of these occasions. Now, as grandparents ourselves, separated by distance from our grandchildren, we keep in touch with letters. We also send them religious videos, and when we are with them on visits, we read Bible stories and pray together. We are supporting what their parents are already doing. But I know this would never have taken place if it hadn't been for the faithfulness of my grandparents when I was growing up. It goes back all the way to when I was a child.

This is third-generation Christianity, and possibly fourth or even further back—who can tell?

In Deuteronomy 6:1-2 (NKJV), God spoke to Moses and commanded that the statutes and judgments be observed and that the people be taught to keep them, so that "you and your son and your grandson, all the days of your life" would have their days prolonged. God's love is actually expressed in law. Love is, in fact, the great principle backing the Law. Salvation itself is a love affair; as we read in John 14:15, if we love Jesus, we will keep His commandments. God has always had the best interests of His children at heart.

Grandparents have a vital role to fill if faith is to be found on the earth when Jesus comes back. In this same Deuteronomy passage we find the familiar words:

> *These commandments that I give you today are to be upon your hearts. Impress them on your children. Talk about them when you sit at home and when you walk along the road, when you lie down and when you get up.*
> (Deuteronomy 6:6-7)

Our obedience is a manifestation of our love. Talking, sitting, walking, lying down, rising up—that's pretty much all the time. Unreserved, wholehearted commitment—that's what God wants. Because the human heart is so fragile, so prone to forget God and His ways. And the lure of the world is strong.

CONSISTENCY

My wise, retired pastor friend, Fred Fels, wrote: "Our love for the Lord and for our grandchildren is the most dramatic way to transmit faith. There is a clearly observable principle that when we are relaxed and natural in our faith, our children and then our grandchildren see Christ in us and choose Him. The other options are, by contrast, less and less appealing."

One grandparent wrote:

Since our love for the Lord permeates everything we do, my husband and I just automatically talk about Him when we are around our grandchildren. Actually, the grandchildren talk about Jesus to us, even if we don't mention Him first. When we are together, I sing songs to the little ones—the same songs which my grandmother and mother sang to me. Some of these are old hymns, some are old ballads, some are just funny old songs, but the children love them. I can keep the grandchildren spellbound just by telling the stories that my grandmother and mother told me. Most of these stories are real-life happenings of our family, like how Grandpa got thrown from his horse and Grandma had to ride 10 miles on horseback to get the doctor, or how my dad walked the aisle at church to rededicate his life, and I saw such a change in him that I decided to invite Jesus into my heart. Our grandchildren are receiving family traditions and learning that God is to be the center of life.

I think cartoonist Bill Keane must have had someone like Pastor Fred and this grandmother in mind when, in his *Family Circus* cartoon, he showed a darling ponytailed girl looking into her grandpa's face and, as she's stroking it, saying, "Our other grandfather's in heaven, but I'm glad we have a grandfather who art on earth."

So, when riding in the car, playing a game, eating out at the grandchild's favorite place, or just taking a walk, we can share how good God is, what a beautiful world He made, how He takes care of us, meets our needs, answers our prayers, gives us friends, and shows His love for us in so many ways. We are building relationships, but more than that, we are helping in faith building. Regardless of the age of the grandchild, as we seize the moment, we are modeling faith.

REVERENCE FOR THE LORD'S DAY

Phyllis Seminoff, my California grandmother friend, speaks of her paternal grandmother with great pride and affection:

In my mind's eye, I can still see myself walking the block or so from my grandparents' home to the Church of the Brethren. It must have been a picture—tiny, impeccably dressed Grandma (who was called Sister Henry at church), with her long gray hair pulled up into the neatest bun, holding the hand of a tiny, talkative five-year-old. Since my parents didn't attend church, Grandma took on the responsibility. To this day, I can remember being proud to be with "Sister Henry," who was known to love the Lord.

But Sunday school and church were only the beginning of our day. After lunch, off we'd go to the Salvation Army service across town. Quite a change of pace, with its vibrant band! Then, Sunday evening, we were back to the quieter service at Grandma's church.

Grandma's whole day was dedicated to the Lord. I remember she wouldn't ever think of cooking, sewing, or doing any type of work on Sunday. Saturday was preparation for Sunday, and she did it all then. What an impression that made on me as a child! I can still hear Grandma saying that Sunday was the Lord's Day and it was not a day of work. It impressed me so that, sixty-plus years later, it's still imprinted on my heart.

There was much Grandma taught me in our churchgoing, from being respectful of the clergy to being a humble person and being willing to wash another's feet, as we did in the Communion service twice a year. These and many more Christian attitudes were implanted in me through Grandma's example.

Reverence for the Lord's Day was something many respondents wrote about. Living as we do in a time when Sunday is no longer observed and respected as God commanded, how important it is that we seek ways to help our grandchildren understand the day God gave for rest. Phyllis and I—and, of course, many others—learned this from the example of our grandparents. Reverence for the Lord's Day is an outward sign of an inward reality, that we are His people.

An old saying goes like this: "Our great-grandfathers called it the holy Sabbath; our grandfathers, the Sabbath; our fathers, Sunday. But today we call it the weekend."

REVERENCE FOR WHAT THE
CHURCH REPRESENTS

One grandmother said that one of the changes in relating our faith to that of our grandchildren today has to do with changes in the manner of worship, particularly music.

> It has been surprising to find that the old hymns are not as dear and familiar to our children and grandchildren today. It is very important, therefore, to become acquainted with the present-day Christian music that is so much a part of our grandchildren's lives. At this point grandparents must learn to be tolerant and willing to change. However, I think that at the same time, in a limited way, a grandparent should try to teach some of the classic hymns to the grandchild as opportunity presents itself.

The subject of contemporary Christian music is a volatile one in many churches. But I think this grandmother has it right. We do need to have an open mind, be tolerant, and be willing to change, difficult as it may be. Listen, sweeping changes occur in every generation. Why should we expect it to be any different now? Charles Swindoll has a terrific chapter on this in his book *Rise and Shine.* He reminds us of Daniel the prophet, who wrote that it is "He [God] who changes times and seasons" (Daniel 2:21). The point being, grandparents, that we must not be so rigid as to turn our grandchildren off by our refusal to accept their preferences. On the other hand, our grandchildren need to be respectful of *our* preferences as well, in regard to music or other things. Those churches that incorporate both kinds of music into their services are finding this to be the best way.

For myself, I am of the old school. I can attest to the beauty and importance of the old hymns. When my husband died and I was getting used to life without him, the words of these beautiful old songs lifted me up as they found their way into my thinking. Those old refrains even now play themselves over in my head, the lyrics washing over me with the peace that only God can provide.

TWO GRANDMOTHERS

The late Reverend Rex Lindquist shared with me his wonderful memories of his Swedish grandmother:

Grandmother Wallin lived the Christian life consistently. Never a cross word or action was seen or heard. She sang the hymns of worship in both Swedish and English. She sat for hours with me, telling the stories of her childhood. I have memories of being with her at her summer cottage on Fishhook Lake. Her Swedish heritage was most evident when she was rowing a boat through stormy waters and when she sat quietly fishing.

As an infant I was very sickly. The doctors and my parents finally gave up in attempting to find medicine to settle my stomach, which refused food. But Grandmother quietly prayed and gave me to the Lord to be His minister. I survived. It wasn't until after I graduated from Northwestern Bible School and entered the ministry that she told me of that prayer.

My Grandmother Lindquist, on father's side of the family, had a great spiritual influence in my life, although I had little contact with her until I enrolled in Bible school and moved into her home in Minneapolis. I remember her reading the Psalms in Swedish every day. I remember her concern for keeping the Lord's day. Her holy life and love and prayers for me left an impression which can never be forgotten.

I still praise the Lord for the heritage which my two grandmothers left for me. What a gift God gave to this boy!

Rex and his lovely wife, Fern, had a mission church in Anchorage, Alaska, and ministered faithfully there for 13 years, leaving in the end only because their aging parents needed care. They then became what they called "book missionaries" through their Christian bookstore. My husband and I enjoyed the privilege of having this godly couple as friends. Rex attributed his deep-seated faith to the influence of his godly grandmothers. Rex was a greatly respected businessman as well as a theologian—a serious-minded man—but he was also one of the sweetest servants of the Lord I've ever known. The people who knew them will never forget Rex and Fern Lindquist.

GRANDMA'S PRAYER CLOSET

You can understand my joy at receiving a response to my questionnaire from a cousin on the paternal side of my family, since I never knew my paternal grandparents. Cousin Gilbert, a retired pastor, revealed things to me I had never heard about our grandmother, including a story oddly similar to Reverend Lindquist's.

My paternal grandfather died in 1913, so memories of him have not surfaced from my relatives. But according to my cousin, I had a godly grandmother who knew how to pray and reach out to God. Grandma Westra lived across the street from him when he was a small child. "When I was two years old, I was very ill with appendicitis and surgery was to be performed," wrote Gil. "Grandma Westra went into her 'prayer closet' and bargained with God that if I might live, I would be His servant and she would see to it that this happened. When the doctor came to the hospital to perform the surgery, a miraculous healing had occurred, and the operation didn't take place."

Wisely, Gilbert's parents and grandma didn't reveal this sequence of events to Gilbert until later in life. "They feared that I might be influenced on decision for ministry just because of Grandma's prayer and not because I felt the call of God in my heart. But what was of interest to me," he explained, "was that ever since I was a small boy, I had the desire to be a minister of the gospel. I always knew that this is what I wanted to do. Later, when the decision was made, my parents revealed Grandma's prayer to me."

Gilbert remembers Grandma Westra remarrying. "He was a kind gentleman with snow-white sideburns, but he died suddenly, and I remember being at grandmother's house during the funeral. I remember the horse-drawn funeral carriage—a glass box on a wagon and the coffin inside—and the procession to the graveyard."

Gilbert's family moved to Minnesota, and our grandmother had to do some long-distance grandparenting without benefit of e-mails or telephone calls. But he remembers coming as a small boy with his father to the little Iowa town where she lived to spend a few days with his grandma in the summertime.

I recall that Grandma laid out our clothes for Sunday on Saturday. One time she laid them out on Friday and I told her it was the wrong day. "No, Gilbert," she said in her thick Dutch drawl. "Yes, Grandma, I'm right," I told her. But she was only convinced when she had me ask the neighbor across the street. I returned like a victorious general, announcing that I was correct. Grandma's response? She put away our Sunday clothes.

I carry such memories with me, too. Sunday was a day to be hallowed (this was the word used). It was to be kept holy. Mother always laid out our Sunday best on Saturday. The shoes were always polished until you could almost see your face in them. Hair was washed, baths taken, food prepared for the next day. Nothing was left for Sunday that couldn't be taken care of on Saturday. And on Sunday we dutifully marched off for two services—morning and afternoon, with Sunday school following. Then it was on to Grandpa and Grandma's house, where all the uncles, aunts, and cousins congregated for tea in the wintertime or lemonade in warm weather, always accompanied by one of Grandma's wonderful delicacies or something Grandpa had bought at the marvelous Dutch bakery in town. These were rituals, important practices, that made an indelible impression on me. Is it any wonder that I have always felt Sundays are special?

I loved playing paper dolls, cutting them out of the big Sears and Montgomery Ward catalogs, but on Sundays the scissors were "*verboten*"—forbidden.

We cousins enjoyed playing yard games, but almost without fail, Grandpa would come outside and say, "You're making too much noise. What will the neighbors think?"

We grew up with the awareness that we were being watched by the next-door neighbors—neighbors whom Grandpa considered to be "worldly." We were to set an example of godly behavior. These things were ingrained in us. To be honest, I've always doubted whether the neighbors even noticed what we were doing. Perhaps Grandpa should have reminded us more often in private of the all-seeing heavenly Father who loved us and wanted us to be mannerly, thoughtful children.

O LORD, You are the portion of my inheritance and my cup;
You maintain my lot.
The lines have fallen to me in pleasant places;
Yes, I have a good inheritance.

—Psalm 16:5-6 (NKJV)

Cousin Gil remembers going with Grandma to an old white-frame church for the Dutch service in the afternoon. "Her large, black skirt had deep pockets, which had peppermints in it for

Gilbert, who might become sleepy," he recalls. "The singing of the Dutch Psalms, especially Psalm 42, nearly raised the rafters!" What Gilbert especially remembers, however, were Grandma's prayers.

I share these memories. On the wall in my home, in a velvet-lined shadowbox, are two Dutch psalmbooks, my mother's and Grandma Brunsting's (my maternal grandmother). The pages are worn and yellowed, evidencing much use. The clasps are filigree gold. My children grew up seeing these old psalmbooks—a legacy from the past, a silent but powerful testimony to a mother and grandmother, praying women. The books have always been a conversation piece, the children and I proudly showing them off. When asked what they represent, I explain that they belonged to my progenitors. Mother and Grandma carried them to church every Sunday and sang from them. They are a reminder of my godly heritage. These women were my Loises.

If Sunday had not been observed as a day of rest during the last three centuries, I have not the slightest doubt that we should have been at this moment a poorer people and less civilized. —THOMAS MACAULAY

3

WHAT A GRANDCHILD WILL DO FOR LOVE

Only take heed to yourself, and diligently keep yourself,
lest you forget the things your eyes have seen, and lest they
depart from your heart all the days of your life. And teach
them to your children and your grandchildren.
—DEUTERONOMY 4:9 (NKJV)

According to his description of himself, he was a greenhorn farm boy who, though transplanted to southern California, was not many years removed from Indiana. "I found the adjustment to city life more than a little difficult. But it wasn't just this—missing the country life—that prompted me, as a 15-year-old, to run away from home in the dead of winter. It wasn't daredevilry; it was plain old homesickness. I was homesick for my grandma. A boy will go a long way for a Grandmother's love. I was starved for love."

That love-starved boy was my husband, Herman Hosier, in 1935. He told his story like this:

Perhaps if I had realized the distance from Highland Park in southern California to Lapel, Indiana (near Indianapolis), and what lay in store for me as I bummed my way across the country in the dead of winter, I might have had second thoughts. But my parents were heavy drinkers and my life was miserable. I received no love, and there came the moment when I couldn't handle it any longer. Back home in Indiana was Grandma and my maiden aunt, Aunt Nell, and there was love.

I left home with only the clothes on my back—a thin sport shirt, worn jeans, and shoes that had already seen enough wear. Tucked under my arm was a flimsy blanket I had hastily pulled from the bed, and in my pocket was my beloved harmonica.

That harmonica went with me wherever I'd go. In Luther Burbank Junior High School, I organized and directed a 30-member harmonica band. We were actually pretty good! So for me to have that harmonica along was no chance thing. I left behind a cap for my head and a jacket, but my trusty harmonica wasn't forgotten. In the long, lonely, bitter-cold days ahead, that harmonica was to prove a lifesaver.

It took three days to get to El Paso, Texas, by freight train. A buddy and I had gone to the freight yards in Los Angeles when we left home. We jumped on a train heading east. By the time we got to El Paso, we hadn't had any food, so we felt pretty weak. I could hardly muster up enough strength and courage to go to the door of a dirty little white house and ask for something to eat. The people were very kind, and since they were eating dinner, they invited us in to share what they had.

Early the next morning, after spending the night in a hobo jungle, we tried to catch a freight going out of El Paso, but instead we were picked up by a railroad bull (a policeman) and taken to jail. Vagrancy was against the law at that time. We were herded into a tank and kept there until early afternoon. Needless to say, I was scared spitless. To bolster my courage, I played my trusty harmonica.

After the court proceeding, the judge took me out and treated me to a free meal. The moment we got out, my friend took off and I never saw him again. (I found out later that he caught a freight going back to Los Angeles.) But I was determined to get to Indiana and told the judge where I was headed and why. He was a kindly man and told me to walk out of town and try thumbing rides on the highway. He explained the dangers of jumping freight trains, that the suction could pull you under, and all the things that could happen.

YOUNG HERMAN THE HOBO

I tried to comply with the judge's wishes, but by the time I had walked to the outskirts of El Paso, it was getting dark. No one was stopping to pick up a bedraggled-looking, skinny kid, and I was sure there were coyotes and wolves just waiting to jump on me. Back to town I went, heading for the freight yards, and I caught the next freight out.

Have you ever thought what it would be like to ride on a fast freight? (They used to call them Red Ball Freights.) I have been told these trains would travel 70 to 75 miles per hour. If the car was empty, you really got bounced around. And since there was no insulation, it got mighty cold, making it impossible to sleep. I knew enough to realize that I had to stay awake and keep moving around or I would freeze to death. It took a long while before we came to another town. I was terribly cold and hungry.

Some of the tramps in El Paso had alerted me to the fact that you could go to the railroad yard and find the building where they heated the sand used to stop the train on icy tracks. A guy could get nice and toasty warm in there. By now the weather had turned bitter cold. It was December.

I was so hungry, however, that I knew that before trying to get warm I must have something to eat. Many times people wouldn't let you inside their homes, nor did they even want you on their door stoop. Often they refused to give you anything. Kids called me names, threw rocks at me, and sicced their dogs on me. However, I recall a Spanish-speaking family who showed kindness to me and stopped the growls in my stomach with good food. After filling my stomach and thanking the people, I made my way back to the railroad and the shed where they were heating the sand. How warm and welcome it was! I was told that a freight was heading toward Indianapolis via East St. Louis, Missouri, early the next morning.

My education about how vagrants lived was increasing. They would steal, but they never refused to share something with another bum. They usually had their "jungles" along the railroad at both ends of town. Here they would pool their resources—potatoes, canned goods, tomatoes, beans, etc.—and make what they called "mulligan stew." There was always a big campfire going to keep you warm, and there was always coffee. All the latest news was shared—what was happening along the railroad route, where you could expect a handout, places to steer away from, and so on.

It was at one such jungle that a kindly older gentleman gave me an overcoat and a cap. I was really grateful.

About four that morning, I caught the freight heading for East St. Louis. What I didn't know, but quickly found out, was that the boxcars were full and the only available place to ride was in the reefers. These were cars used to haul vegetables. On either side of the car were compartments from top to bottom that held ice in the summer to keep the produce from spoiling. In the winter the ice compartments were empty—you had to climb up the ladder on the outside of the car, lift the lid at the top, and crawl in. There was just enough room for a skinny kid like myself, but once inside, you had to make sure the lid didn't slam shut. If it did, you were a goner. (I later heard about men who had died that way.) But the old hobos told me what to do if I ever found myself needing to use one of those compartments, and I followed their instructions.

I rode in this car for about 12 hours. It was so cramped and cold, and I was so hungry. I comforted myself by reminding myself that it wouldn't be too much longer and I'd be with Grandma and Aunt Nell. Finally the train chugged to a stop in the mammoth rail yard of East St. Louis. I was so cold that I barely managed to climb out.

I hadn't walked very far when I came to a little railroad shanty. I could see smoke coming out of a chimney, and I knew there was a warm fire inside. I knocked at the door. There was no answer, so I went in, took off my heavy overcoat, and sat down. It was my feet that were especially cold. I took off my shoes, and no wonder my feet were freezing—there were big holes in both soles. Some newspapers lay on the little table, so I tore pieces off and stuffed my shoes until there was just enough room to get my feet back in.

After getting warm, I pulled out my harmonica and started to play, hoping to dispel my hunger, my thirst, and my loneliness. Suddenly the door opened and in walked the switchmen. They looked at me in surprise! It's one thing to find seasoned old bums along the tracks, but I had the feeling they didn't often encounter a kid like me. I think they would have thrown me out, but they felt sorry for me. They asked a lot of questions, and I answered them truthfully. "I'm on my way to a little town outside Indianapolis. My grandma lives there, and since things weren't so good at home, I figured I'd go to her. I know she'll let me stay." Did I detect tears in one fellow's eyes?

HUNGRY

They asked me to play some more songs on the harmonica. "Where did you learn to play that thing like that?" one of the men asked.

"I don't know," I said. "I've always played my harmonica. Guess I taught myself."

"Are you hungry?" the man who blinked away the tears asked. He fished in his pocket, as did the other man, placing in my hand a fistful of money. Then they told me where the nearest restaurant was. "When you finish eating, you come back. We'll take you to the roundhouse." (The roundhouse was a big building where the engines were driven to a table where they could be turned around.)

"Yeah, come on back so we can hear some more of that harmonica," one of the guys said as he patted me on the back.

That felt good. I was encouraged. I needed it!

At about 11:30 that night, the switchmen took me to the roundhouse. My new friends told the men in there about me. "You're a pretty spunky kid," one man said.

"Going to your grandma's, huh? Does she know you're on the way?"

I hadn't thought about that, but I knew it didn't matter. Grandma would be glad to see me. I knew that. I remembered how hard it had been for her to kiss me good-bye when we'd left for California. She was a wonderful lady. I could hardly wait to get back to her.

"Play the harmonica for these guys, Herm," the man who had emptied his pocket of change requested. So they all sat around for about 15 minutes while I entertained them. They clapped, slapped me on the back, and wished me well. That felt good too.

Then things started happening. One fellow walked over to his locker and pulled out his lunch bag; another gave me a heavy railroad jacket; someone else gave me a pair of overshoes. All of them emptied their pockets, stuffing change in my pockets. "There's a freight pulling out for Indianapolis in 15 minutes. Let's go," one man said.

I thanked everyone and we took off. The men rushed me to a waiting switch engine. We stood on the front platform in front of the cowcatcher and rode about two miles to where the train was getting ready to leave. They rushed me to an empty boxcar, opened the door, shoved me in, wished me good luck, and they were gone.

AND OH, SO COLD!

Since I had just eaten and had some warm coffee in my stomach, I lay down in a corner, pulled the old coat over me, and fell asleep. I don't know how long I slept, but the train slowing down awakened me. I felt stiff as a board, and oh, I was so cold! I remembered that in one of the pockets of the railroad jacket there were some funny papers rolled up. I took out a match and lit the papers and tried to warm my hands. As you probably know, rolled up papers don't burn well and also emit a horrible smell. I blew the last sparks out and threw them in a corner. By this time the train had come to a complete stop. I slid open the heavy car door, leaped out, and found we had pulled over on a siding.

About this time a man came from the back end of the train and was heading toward a shanty down the way. He asked if I was cold, and through jittering jaws I managed to say, "Yes."

"Get in the caboose," he instructed as he headed for the shanty. Shortly he came back. He was furious. "Did you light a fire in the boxcar?" I had to tell him yes, but he wouldn't listen to my explanation. He came rushing toward me and pushed me out of the caboose. About that time the train started up. There I stood in the middle of the tracks, not knowing what to do.

The moon was shining brightly on the sparkling snow. All of a sudden, I was scared. I broke down for the first time since leaving home, and I cried like a baby. I felt so alone. Who loved me? Who cared what happened to me? "Grandma, Grandma," I cried. "I need you. Where are you? Am I going to make it?"

I stumbled my way toward the shanty. About a quarter of a mile down the railroad tracks, I saw the figure of a man standing in the middle of the tracks. He asked my name and wanted to know if I was the kid who lit a fire in the boxcar. (I figured out that the man in the caboose had telegraphed the shanty, told them what had happened, and said that they'd better watch for me.) I said yes and told him what had actually happened. He was kind and said I could spend the night with him.

The next morning this kindly man took me home with him. When we got to his house, I could see why he had befriended me. He had four children of his own. The lady of the house fed me a scrumptious breakfast. The father then gave me a lecture on the dangers of riding the rails in the middle of winter. "Son, many men lose their lives, or they are badly maimed as they slip on the ice and snow while trying to board a train. I want you to try hitchhiking on the highways."

Before I left, he looked at my feet, told me to take

off the old shoes I had, and put heavy-duty railroad shoes on my feet. They were about two sizes too big, but he stuffed them so my feet wouldn't slide, and they felt warm and sturdy. I thanked them for all they had done and walked on down the highway.

Once again I was trying what hadn't worked before. I walked and walked and walked some more. It seemed as though hundreds of cars passed by. Then about three or four that afternoon, a big truck and trailer stopped. I climbed aboard. I was so grateful. How good it was to get off my feet!

While en route, the driver asked me many questions, and I tried to answer them honestly. "Heading for your Grandma's, huh? Grandmas are pretty special. Yeah, what would we do without Grandmas!"

Since I didn't have any money, he said the thing to do would be to find out where the jail was when I entered each town. "These towns don't like vagrants on the street at night. The jails will give you a meal, a bunk to sleep on in a cell, and they will lock you up. But they'll feed you the next morning and turn you loose. Since you'll be turning yourself in, they won't write anything up on you. Do it, son. It's the only way you're going to make it to Indianapolis." I guess he could see I was pretty emaciated and that I was really tired.

That night I did what he said. It sounded like a fair deal. The food tasted good, though when they locked me up, it gave me a panicky feeling. But the truck driver was right. I'd never have made it if I hadn't followed his advice. And three and a half weeks from the time I'd left home, I arrived at my Grandmother's home.

GRANDMA!

I knew I was really dirty and that I looked awful. My feet were so sore. (I found out later that they were badly frostbitten.) But now that I had reached Grandma's, I didn't know whether to go to the front door or the back door. I decided, since I was so dirty, I'd better go in the back door, remembering how clean Grandma and Aunt Nell were.

Timidly, I knocked on the back door. What awaited me?

Grandma answered the knock. She stared at this dirty tramp, not recognizing me at first. I was a sight, and I'd grown taller since she'd last seen me a couple of years earlier. Who was this dirty, skinny, lanky kid at her back door? Then I spoke up. "Hello, Grandma."

She screamed out, "Oh, dear God, it's little Herman!" (I was always called "Little Herman," since I was named after my uncle, a big man.) Aunt Nell came running.

Grandma threw her arms around me, hugging and kissing me, dirt and all. Then Aunt Nell had her turn. I felt so loved. Yeah, a boy will go a long way for love. In fact, it doesn't matter how young or old you are, there's nothing like love, is there?

TOWN HERO

That's my husband's story. I couldn't hear him tell it, and I couldn't write it, without weeping. Wherever we went and he gave his testimony, the audience was in tears too. Oh, how much we all need to be loved!

Someone has said: "Let's bring back grandmothers—the old-fashioned kind, who take you by the hand and lead you into the future, who are safe and savvy and smarter than your mother." Oh, how I agree! And I'm sure you'd agree also. But there's a little more to my husband's story, and only he could tell it like it really happened:

> Once I was inside Grandma's immaculately clean house, Grandma and Aunt Nell made the discovery that my clothes were covered with lice. They filled their old washtub with water. Did a bath ever feel so good! Grandma yelled through the door, "Herman, your clothes will have to be burned. I can't stand the possibility of having lice around."
>
> Suddenly, I remembered my harmonica. I jumped out of the tub, stuck my head out the door, and called out, "Grandma, be sure and fish my harmonica out of the jacket pocket."
>
> I hadn't found the Lord as yet, but this I know now (and I think I understood it then in some way): Grandma's God had been watching over me. Grandma said I sure must have kept my guardian angels busy those weeks I was trying to make it across country to get back to her.

In the weeks that followed, Herman Hosier became the town hero. He was kept busy telling his story in one place after another, and always he kept his trusty harmonica handy. If it wasn't the mayor, it was some civic club calling upon him to share his experience and play his harmonica.

A GRANDMOTHER'S FAITH

He enrolled in school, and it was decided that he should stay with his grandmother and aunt. He never lacked for love; Grandma and Aunt Nell saw to that. But Grandma did more than love this grandson of hers. Every night, she sat in her old rocker reading her Bible, and she made sure that Herman heard the Word of God. She spoke to him often about the Lord, telling him that he needed God's love in his heart and that God's love would enable him to lead a good life. Often she would remind him that God had spared his life. The good seed of the Word was faithfully sown in young Herman's heart.

In the summer he became a hired hand on a farm. The hiring lady was a Christian who carried on where Grandma had left off. At mealtimes she saw to it that there was a tract or a portion of a gospel at Herman's plate. He began to read on his own, looking forward to the next portion of the gospel that this dear saint would tuck alongside his plate.

After he had been in Lapel, Indiana, for two years, his parents pleaded with his grandmother to send him back home. Letters and phone calls were exchanged. Herman's parents promised they would give up drinking if he would only come home. Reluctantly, Herman, now 17, agreed to return home. It was difficult to leave. The love he'd received from his beloved grandma and his Aunt Nell had met a tremendous need in his young life. This time he rode the rails as a paying passenger:

> I was back home a week before Christmas, and sure enough, my parents kept their word for a week. Then at Christmastime they started drinking again.
>
> Shortly after this, I started playing the violin and my harmonica in a cowboy dance band. I also sang for this group. I was an all-around musician at heart.
>
> Then one of my buddies in my last year of high school prevailed upon me to substitute at their church in a musical group. It was a little Friends church, and I literally sat on the edge of my seat as I heard the gospel faithfully preached. One Sunday, when the pastor gave the altar call, I jumped up and actually ran down the aisle to give my heart to the Lord. My harmonica and I got converted, and I never went back to the ways of the world.
>
> Grandma had sown the seed, the little old hired lady on the farm had helped tend and nurture it, and my buddy, his Christian friends and his family, and the pastor at that little church watered that seed of the Word until it took root in my heart. Now I really knew the meaning of love. Praise God, Grandma's faith became my faith!

In the years that followed, Herman went to missions in downtown Los Angeles with his harmonica, playing and singing, using the beautiful tenor voice God had gifted him with as he shared his faith with the down-and-outers on Los Angeles's skid row. It was there that he was heard singing by someone who invited him to substitute one Sunday for the Old Fashioned Revival Hour Quartet. After that, he was a regular in the choir and with the quartet, ministering with Dr. Charles E. Fuller, founder of a radio program heard internationally.

Still later, Herman became lead tenor and soloist with the well-known Haven of Rest Quartet. And he became producer of *The Haven of Rest* broadcast from Hollywood, California, serving the Lord in that capacity for 17 years, traveling across the continent and throughout Canada, sharing his testimony and singing. He was a charter member of the Baptist Laymen's Male Chorus and sang with them on the radio for 10 years. He was a participant in recording dozens of gospel records and sang under the direction of Ralph Carmichael in his orchestra. He served as minister of music in many churches throughout southern California while still singing with these groups.

Herman was a dear man of God who traced the awakening of desire to know about the Lord to his faithful grandmother. Yes, a fellow will go a long way for love. That journey in his 15th year, difficult as it was, led him to knowledge of the Lord of love. And that journey, which introduced him to Christ and the Bible, made it possible for him to go on to become a dedicated servant of the Lord for the rest of his life.

God greatly used Herman in singing His praises, with his voice and testimony being heard around the world. And all through the years, he played his harmonica. No one could play the old tunes and gospel songs better than Herman the Harmonicat! I am almost certain that God asked Herman to sing, direct a heavenly choir, and play the equivalent of a heavenly harmonica when he got to heaven. And of course, Grandma and Aunt Nell—as well as his parents, whom he led to the Lord—were all there rejoicing with him in the presence of the Lord.

Addendum: Herman and I were married February 14, 1974. We were sweethearts for the 21 years of our marriage—a God-blessed marriage that found us ministering for the Lord in many places throughout the country.

Herman served in the Korean War, using his musical gifts and knowledge of the Word to conduct chapel services for the men on the field. He used his G.I. benefits to get an education at Pepperdine College, obtaining degrees in music and education. When his voice became weakened by so many years of use, he turned to education and became a Christian school principal.

Herman was wonderful with children. He became a grandfather figure to hundreds of children through the years. His love and influence were greatly used as he continued to share his story and as he helped parents and grandparents realize the need to nurture faith in their children and grandchildren.

Between us, we had 15 grandchildren. How he enjoyed them!

It was Good Friday, April 14, 1995, at noon, when God called Herman to his heavenly home. It was instantaneous cardiac arrest. His spirit left him and we know he heard the words "Well done, Herman, good and faithful servant. Enter into the joy of the Lord!"

In his last four years, Herman dedicated himself to daily, diligent prayer on behalf of all our family, our friends, and needs that were brought to his attention. He faithfully kept his prayer diary, and when God answered his prayers, he praised the Lord and crossed those needs off his list. He spent six hours (if not more) in daily prayer and Bible study. He was a personification of Christ's love.

4

A PROFOUND INFLUENCE

[God] chooses our inheritance for us.
—PSALM 47:4 (NASB)

David, a darling three-year-old, and his mother, Janet, were shopping. David gravitated to the spinning stand of cheap plastic toys, but he knew, even at three, not to beg his mother for such junk. As Janet told me, another three-year-old was fussing loudly and demanding one of the toys from the rack. The mother ignored him. As Janet watched, her son inched closer to the boy and said, "You should go to the store with your grandma."

Such wisdom! We grandparents are a soft touch, aren't we? Who can resist the charms of these little sweethearts?

I remember seeing a cartoon in which a little fellow is saying, "I make money the old-fashioned way. I butter up Grandma!" We smile at that, but loving and giving are synonymous, especially when it comes to our grandchildren. Hopefully, our grandchildren don't use us or think of us only as having deep pockets!

Shortly after we moved back to California to be near one of our daughters and her husband and children, the grandchildren were helping us unpack. It was like Christmas for them, unwrapping all the carefully wrapped dishes and glassware. The girls were already 10 and 13, but we showed them how to go about the unpacking. We had a lot of fun, even though it was work and we had to be careful with the fragile things. Many of the items had a story connected to them. "This was Grandma Hattie's special cut-glass bowl. Grandma Hattie was my mother, your mother's grandma. This belonged to my grandmother …" And so it went.

When it came time for the girls to leave, I wanted to reward them. Their mother protested and so did they. Still, we managed to slip a little something into their hands. Later, however, I found a note folded on my desk. Inside, it read:

Grandma, I don't want your money, I just want your love.
    Love, Christa

She'd put the dollar bill I'd given her with the note. Well, yes, I cried! We'd missed the grandchildren so much during those years when we'd lived in another state. Often, then, we'd thought about what it would be like living nearby so we could participate in the events in their lives. And now we were doing it! We could truly experience the *grand* in being grandparents.

"Special and of Value to God"

One 59-year-old grandmother wrote to tell about her grandson and his third-grade class who had to show and tell what they liked to do the best with their grandparents for grandparents' day at school. "We were there, of course," this grandmother wrote, "and J. D. had drawn a picture of Grandpa, Grandma, and himself at the Kmart store, as if we were shopping. I have the picture in my cedar chest, which contains the many precious treasures of our grandchildren. We've taken him shopping ever since he was old enough to sit in the shopping cart." Of course that would be his favorite thing; he'd been doing it for a few years already with his much-loved grandparents.

Many children, however, don't have grandmas and grandpas nearby who can take them along on shopping excursions. They are the grandparents who have to grandparent in absentia. When we were numbered among them, my daughter wrote:

> Because I see how deprived our children are in not having you, as grandparents, near, I am answering your questionnaire. God intended for families to be together—to strengthen each other, for grandparents to help fill in the gaps, to see needs and fulfill them for one another, to care for and nurture each other. Being together as a family, living within proximity, seeing each other a couple times a week, doing favors for each other, loving, giving, thoughtfulness in words and deeds—how valuable all this is to children. Do you realize what a profound influence

that is? It provides that staying sense of belonging. If there was only one thing I could say about how all-important my grandparents were, and how they influenced me, I would say they gave me that sense of belonging, of security. We were family. And with that came a sense of respect and love and self-worth and a sense that I was special and of value to them and God.

My daughter's sentiments were voiced similarly in many respondents' stories. The letters came from all over the country. Friends looked back fondly, reminiscing about the influence of their grandparents.

Jean Dickson, a grandmother in Frisco, Texas, spoke of her paternal grandmother in such a loving way.

Grandmother shared her faith and values in a way that was never pushy. She just lived the life so well that not much else had to be said. She suffered the loss of two daughters when they were young, which was very painful for her, but I never heard her complain. She took three grandchildren to raise as her own even though it was during the Depression and times were very hard. Her stability and strength were comforting to me as a child. She had so many grandchildren, but she would find a way to single me out and make me feel special.

Jean also has wonderful memories of her maternal grand-parents. Although she didn't get to know her maternal grand-father, she heard such good things about him that she could say:

> I have gained much comfort in my life just knowing that I am part of him. He had a wonderful reputation, according to everyone who knew him. But my maternal grandmother was something else—she possessed the spirit of a true pioneer. She wasn't afraid of anything, or so it always seemed to me as a child and, I must say, even still today. Always a snuff dipper, she said that from the moment she was saved, she was delivered and never had any desire to try snuff again.
>
> This grandmother faced much hardship and painful experiences during her lifetime but always came through with grace and strength. She nursed my grandfather through his long and painful injury. (He was a master carpenter and fell from the roof of a schoolhouse. This was before today's miracle drugs and penicillin, and he got an infection that lasted for three painful years, eventually causing his death.) Then grandmother lost her youngest daughter to cancer at age 24 and took her five-year-old grand-daughter to raise. The strength she showed has had an immeasurable impact on me throughout my life. When things are hard for me, I remember Grandma's courage and faith.

Years after everyone else was cooking with gas and burning electric lights, she still preferred kerosene lamps and her old woodstove. The smell of her buttermilk biscuits baking in a woodstove still lingers in my mind. The nights spent in her comfortable old house, the walks in the woods with her, picking violets or cutting a Christmas tree, are wonderful memories.

These grandparents had a profound impact on my life.

GRANDPARENTING IN ABSENTIA

One of the things that surfaced with the most frequency in the responses I received was the heartache grandparents experience from grandparenting in absentia. "If only we weren't so far away," they said. "It's not easy to grandparent by long distance." I sensed the emotion behind those words. I understood only too well. At one time we were separated from our 15 grandkids scattered across the country. It's true, long-distance grandparents don't get to experience that special kind of joy that comes from taking a little one by the hand and walking into the store, lifting him into the cart, and watching as his eyes light up when he spies the spinning stand of toys.

I remember one shopping excursion in particular, with my daughter Rhonda and five-year-old Christa at Macy's department store. Rhonda had an armful of garments to try on, and when we reached the fitting room, she proceeded to hang them up. Then she reached for her shoulder-strap purse and found it was missing. Quickly, we went in opposite directions, retracing our steps. Christa went with me. We didn't find the purse, so we headed back up the escalator to meet my daughter. She was coming down and had a happy look on her face. As we saw each other, Rhonda pointed to the purse hanging on her shoulder.

Christa tugged at my hand. "Grandma, you know why she found it, don't you?"

I knew, but I wanted to hear it from her. Bending over, I replied, "Tell me, honey."

"She found it 'cuz I prayed to God to keep it safe till Mama got there. God can be trusted. You know that, don't you, Grandma?"

Long-distance grandparents don't get to experience such events very often, nor the fun that comes from getting up early, loading the fishing gear in the car, and taking off for the lake for some early morning fishing with one's grandson and his golden retriever.

We feel deprived, too, of church and school programs, of picnics, of trips to the zoo, the mountains, or the beach, of baking and cooking—the growing-up events in our grandchildren's lives. Grandparents whose grandchildren don't live nearby miss much of that. But there are things these grandparents can do, and are doing, to make up for that.

INSPIRATION AND ENCOURAGEMENT

Adult grandchildren wrote with deep reverence about their memories of their grandparents. "My maternal grandmother lived with us after the death of her husband, my grandfather," wrote one. "She was an inspiration to all her grandchildren, and I can still hear her say, 'Don't worry, the Lord will provide for all our needs.' Grandma was always at home for us as our mother worked. Grandma was our encourager."

"Inspiration" and "encouragement" were two words frequently mentioned in the questionnaire responses. This came as no surprise to me. But I *was* surprised to hear how many grandmothers and grandfathers were invited to live in the homes of their children as they became widows or widowers and it became evident that they should no longer live alone. I was even more surprised to learn how much such an arrangement proved to be a blessing to everyone, especially the grandchildren.

Alexandra Stoddard wrote that her mother, upon becoming a grandmother, metamorphosed from a gray moth into a radiant butterfly made brilliant by her love.

As mothers, we learn on the job, advancing through our mistakes, but a grandmother is a seasoned professional. Stoddard puts it in good perspective:

> Grandchildren become a grandmother's second chance to mother, without all the day-to-day responsibilities for discipline. This allows her to make more room to allow her grandchildren to be themselves. As a monarch butterfly, her colors dazzle as she flutters around her grandchildren lightheartedly, landing here and there with grace.[1]

> As I watch women with their grandchildren, many seem to have an air of peace and serenity exclusive to the province of grandmotherhood—and indeed it does seem a more spiritual place.   —ALEXANDRA STODDARD[2]

A NATION IN TRANSIT

Today, the special feeling that accompanied living in a small, closely knit community is missing for many. There was a time when children were born and raised in a community, married someone from the community, and lived there all their lives. But times change. Children go off to college, meet their mate, marry, and live elsewhere. Children move into careers that take them away. World War II brought many such changes. We are a nation in transit. No longer can we sing those old words, "Over the river and through the woods, to Grandmother's house we go...."

But sometimes it's not only distance that separates us from loved ones. Recently, I saw a TV program in which grandmothers of grandchildren who were born addicted to drugs cried openly as they pleaded for the right to participate in the lives of these innocent grandchildren. One grandmother I spoke with, between sobs, said, "If grandmothers don't take care of these grandchildren, we are going to have a lost generation." That's scary, and we know it's happening.

A day-care administrator told me, "What children are looking for is a hug, a lap, a kind word, a touch, someone to read them a story, somebody to smile and share with."

For many years my husband was a school principal. He would come home and tell of the little children who literally clung to his long legs. "Starved for love," he would say. He told of one darling little girl who, upon seeing him one morning, ran into his outspread arms, gave him a big hug, and then, when he put her down, clung to his legs, looked up at him, and proudly exclaimed, "I love you, Mr. Hosie, and you're my daddy!" Yes, that brought tears.

With millions of children growing up in homes bereft of two loving parents and deprived of normal family relationships, including the loving, nurturing presence of grandparents, the need for us, as grandparents, to recognize our role becomes increasingly clear.

Whether we are grandparenting by long distance and only get to see our children and grandchildren infrequently, or whether we are fortunate enough to be living near our families, the challenge is to be the kind of grandparents who nurture our relationships so that we can influence the lives of our grandchildren for time and eternity.

The challenge is to give clear signals about what is important in life. Once more I remind myself, as much as you, that the need is to model faith. The Old Testament book of Exodus portrays Moses giving the Israelites the ordinance from God to observe Passover as a way to pass along a legacy to their children and grandchildren by telling them all that the Lord had done for them (12:24-27).

Edith Schaeffer puts it this way in her book *What Is a Family?:*

The plea of God is to *keep* handing down the true truth.... God's direct word comes to us—consider your place in the family as central.... Don't let a gap come because of you. Don't take the beauty of family life— and the reality of being able to hand down true truth to one more generation—as a light thing. It is one of the central commands of God.[3]

Indeed, ours is a profound influence and one we cannot take lightly.

5

A POWERFUL FORCE

He who fears the Lord has a secure fortress,
and for his children it will be a refuge.
—PROVERBS 14:26

Dale Evans Rogers, beloved mother of six, grandmother of 14, and great-grandmother of 33, now with the Lord, spoke movingly of grandparents as being "a powerful force." She pointed out some years ago that in all the reams that have been written on families, parenting, and marriage, grandparents have often been ignored. "I'm here to shout, 'Hey, we're important,'" she wrote.[1]

And so we are. We are more important than even we realize, and we are certainly more important than we are often given credit for.

We're not all ancient, either. While many respondents to my questionnaire wrote about their memories of white-bearded grandfathers who were the venerated patriarchs of their families, others wrote about their own contemporary grandparenting styles. This diversity clearly shows the powerful force that grandparents have been and are.

What can grandparents do? Grandparents can change the world. —DALE EVANS ROGERS

In Dale's autobiograhical book *A Woman at the Well,* the publisher called her "an extraordinary woman of faith," and she certainly was just that. She wrote movingly about her beloved maternal grandmother and the impact of this woman's faith on her own life. Telling about her grandmother's death, she remembered the older woman's beauty and how her mother had difficulty in keeping Dale from standing beside the casket and staring at her grandmother.

> I read in a book or magazine [that] the two most beautiful things in life are to be seen at the extremes of life: the laughter of a child and the look of peace on the face of one who has just died in faith. That look was on [Grandmother's] face; it was the product of long years of love. She had known the travail and trouble of a mother with seven girls and one boy, but with it all she brought them up in faith and she left her faith in their hearts.[2]

She wrote about her great-grandfather, whom she remembered as "a crusty, unconventional and completely lovable old rebel who went his own way and stood on his own feet—no matter what." She knew she inherited her love of fun from him, "and I know that his non-conformity rubbed off on me—generously. Even when he was wrong, there was something delightful about his refusal to conform, or to do whatever everybody else did and expected him to do."[3]

Dale and I corresponded about her memories and about the importance of godly grandparents influencing the younger generation. She idolized her Grandfather Wood. "From the start there was between us that rare spark of understanding and affection that adds such richness to life. He was old, but he never lost his youthfulness or his love for children and young people."[4]

She spoke fondly, too, of her paternal grandparents and of the open Bibles in both grandparents' homes:

> ...well worn and always open. Family prayers were as regular as the meals on the table. How grateful I am for that! And how I pity the child who doesn't have it! There's no telling how far I would have fallen, later, without this undergirding of Christian love and teaching. "Remember thy creator in the days of thy youth." As the twig is bent, so grows the tree.

Dale was a wise woman of God, a devoted mother and grandmother, greatly used wherever she went. These words about her grandparents show how they impacted her life well beyond her childhood. She had a Eunice-like mother, too, whom she said loved her and stayed with her, regardless of her waywardness. Dale described her mother as

> suffering with me in my self-imposed dilemmas—keeping the faith that some day I would come to myself and back to Him. Had she lost her faith in God and in me … I can't even bear the thought of what might have happened to me. (This is why I go up and down the land "witnessing." I urge Christians, young and old, to be faithful to God, persevering in prayer on behalf of those they love—never despairing, never doubting that God, like a good parent, is willing and able to do abundantly more than we ask.)[5]

Her strong voice speaks today even though she and her forbears are no longer living. Dale shows the need to hold on to the faith that characterized the lives of godly grandparents and a faith-filled, praying mother.

MEMORIES

The following terms were used by my respondents in reminiscing about the influence of their godly grandparents. Many were repeated over and over. See if your grandchildren could make these statements about you:

- "I always knew they would help me in any way they could."
- "Very enthusiastic, kind, loving people."

- "Always had a big smile just for me."
- "Ardent and loyal churchgoing people."
- "Always kept close to the Lord, whether it was sunshiny or stormy in their lives."
- "We saw the Golden Rule lived and practiced in their lives."
- "I learned at an early age that my grandpa's partner in business was God."
- "Grandpa had a wonderful sense of humor." (Many respondents spoke of a sense of humor in their grandfathers and how much they loved it and hoped it had rubbed off on them.)
- "Grandpa was a spiritually happy man." (Isn't that a great way to think of it?)
- "My grandfather believed in the Bible as the force within and the power behind his life."
- "Grandma was an amazing woman! I've never seen anyone who possessed a greater spirit of gentle kindness."
- "Grandma was a person of great conviction. The principles she held could not be compromised. She had hope as firm as her convictions."
- "My maternal grandparents reached out to others who were hurting or had financial needs."
- "We learned early from our grandparents that if you loved someone, you wanted to help them."

A SPECIAL TRUST

In the more than one hundred questionnaire responses I received, I saw a consistent theme. Those who responded were individuals whose lives had benefited from the powerful influence of godly grandparents and they were anxious to share their memories. They understood the need for familial faith to be passed on from one generation to another. As a result, they viewed their parenting as a God-given privilege and responsibility, and now as boomer grandparents and even gen-X grandparents, they saw their roles as a special trust—a means whereby they could have a profound influence and be a powerful force for good in the lives of their grandchildren, thus perpetuating strong faith. They understood the meaning of these words: "Let the word of Christ dwell in you richly as you teach ... one another with all wisdom" (Colossians 3:16a).

One young father, on the occasion of his grandparents' 60th anniversary, sent a videotape on which he sought to express his feelings. David Rowe, grandson of Laurence and Gertrude Farr, said:

> It's hard for me to say all that I feel about how I should honor you. I inherited a legacy from the two of you that is just so deeply significant in my life, especially in my growth in godliness, because I look to you, Grampa Farr, as a real model, and to the two of you as a model of what it means to have a Christian marriage.
>
> From my earliest memories of you, Grampa, I remember you as having a love for the Scriptures and a real depth of intimacy in your prayers to God, your life of communication with Him. That has always inspired me. Right now, for instance, we as a family are prepar-

ing to go to Mexico and experience missions in a Third World context. So I'm thinking of the love that you have for the Scriptures and that, because of the faith of our fathers and grandfathers that has been handed down to us, we have discovered what it means to live biblically, to live out of the Bible and follow Jesus—and because of that, we have chosen to spend the summer going to a place like Mexico.

David's heritage—the legacy to which he referred—goes a long way back to his Quaker ancestors, on both sides, who were among the settlers in the Massachusetts Bay Colony between the years 1630 and 1650. His forefathers were missionaries to Jamaica.

David's mother, in speaking of the anniversary event of her parents that prompted her son to reflect on his grandparents' role and the godly legacy they left, wrote:

The members of a godly home are carried on from generation to generation. So children and grandchildren remember the Farrs, their maternal grandparents. The children recall parents on their knees every night (to this day, when it grows more painful each night, that final prayer of the day is still beside the bed on bended knee). They remember a father who could not read tender Bible stories without tears and who wept when he read the beautiful children's story of Heidi learning to trust "the dear Lord" at the feet of a dear old grandmamma.

They remember that giving thanks at the table (when people really ate together at meals three times a day) was a family affair, each one having a turn to pray. But Sunday morning was different—then the grace at breakfast was a song: "Safely Through Another Week." Indeed, they remember that godly heritage. As children and grandchildren, we can truly say, "The lines have fallen to me in pleasant places; Indeed, my heritage is beautiful to me" (Psalm 16:6, NASB).

A child is a person who is going to carry on what you have started. He is going to sit where you are sitting, and when you are gone, attend to those things which you think are important. You may adopt all the policies you please, but how they are carried out depends on him. He will assume control of your cities, states, and nations. He is going to move in and take over your churches, schools, universities and corporations…. The fate of humanity is in his hands.   —ABRAHAM LINCOLN

6

A GRANDFATHER
OF FAITH

One generation will commend your works to another;
they will tell of your mighty acts.
—PSALM 145:4

When Dr. Orrin Bowman, professor at Bethel College, South Bend, Indiana, shared with me some years ago that one of his students had written a life learning paper on the rich legacy her grandfather had left for his loved ones, I was immediately interested. I contacted Linda Van Dyke and learned that her grandfather, Harold F. Haenes, was known for his quotes, his messages of wisdom, the little sayings that flowed from his inner spirit, and his perception of what constituted the good life. He shared these through what became known as the "wayside pulpit" (a roadside bulletin board) in South Bend for 55 years, where his testimony of love, faith, goodness, the importance of family relationships, love of work, visions of heaven, and love for his wife and family had an incalculable impact on all who knew him and read these outdoor messages (which were changed weekly). Linda wrote that she would always be grateful to have been blessed with a grandfather such as this man. One of his sayings reflected the way he felt about grandchildren: "Grandchildren are the jewels of life, a crown of beauty that shines among the riches of life."

In a way, Linda's grandfather is representative of the unnumbered thousands of grandfathers whose stories will never appear in print. Some of you reading this could substitute your grandfather's name in this account. What follows is from Linda's life learning paper:

> When I was a child, my grandfather sat me on his lap and offered me love and acceptance. He had the power to demand respect from our relationship and taught me respect for others. I always knew I was loved and accepted with grandfather.
>
> My grandfather never missed church. His approach to church attendance was philosophical, based on Ephesians 3:14-19:
>
> > *I bow my knees before the Father, from whom every family in heaven and on earth derives its name, that He would grant you, according to the riches of His glory, to be strengthened with power through His Spirit in the inner man; so that Christ may dwell in your hearts through faith; and that you, being rooted*

and grounded in love, may be able to comprehend
with all the saints what is the breadth and length and
height and depth, and to know the love of Christ
which surpasses knowledge, that you may be filled up
to all the fullness of God. (NASB)

Church was important to him, and the faithful teaching of the Word, and he wanted it to be important to his grandchildren. He was a true patriarch. I learned from him a lesson about the value of Sunday church and family togetherness that has lasted ever since. My entire extended family of aunts, uncles, and cousins all attended the same church, and after a service, we would congregate at Grandmother and Grandfather's house. My grandmother's Sunday meals made Sunday even better. Grandpa loved to sit in his favorite chair after one of those big meals and just watch all of us. He always had a smile on his face. I never knew if it was from eating too much or because he just loved to watch his grandchildren.

His prayers at mealtime were more than just a tradition. I learned to pray from my grandfather. I learned that a simple prayer of thanksgiving said honestly is effective in daily life.

The world's problems were important to him, but he always let us know we came first. Our relationships with him were very important to him. What a treasured memory those prayers are now!

I learned at an early age that my grandpa's partner was

God. He was a sign painter by trade. His ability to make letters fascinated me as a child. I would sit by his drawing board for hours and watch his sable brushes make curves, lines, dots of color, and beautiful shapes. He knew how to make money at his trade, but he always gave God credit for whatever came his way and paid what was rightly due to God and then some. "Give one-tenth to God," he taught me. He had a marvelous sense of giving. His understanding of faith and trust in the Lord was the guide to his life. He never doubted God and practiced his beliefs daily.

I was only six when a terrible accident happened to Suzy, a little friend of mine, in which she was burned. She had no hair or eyelashes left. She had only blotches of skin on her back. She had stubs for fingers and melted fingernails. They said she looked like raw meat, so severe was the burning from the accident. My grandfather drew pictures for her and made her laugh. He helped her parents financially and emotionally. I remember how much they looked to him for support. It made an impression on me, even at my young age, and I decided that I wanted to have that kind of influence on others who hurt.

The time came when Suzy needed special shoes to learn to walk again. There was no money, and the shoes were expensive. They had to be specially made. "Girlie shoes," Grandpa called them, and he saw to it that she had them. How fast Suzy learned to walk again in those shiny shoes! The shoes encouraged her performance. Today Suzy is 45 years old and she still tells the shoe story. The scars healed in time, but the strength that went into her shiny shoes sent a special message to many people. The message was faith in practice.

Grandpa was a nurturer, a solid man of God. "Give and it shall be given unto you," he would say, and I knew he was quoting from the Bible. Then he would add, "Give and give until you can give no more." I want to be like my Grandpa!

Grandpa had a wonderful sense of humor. He was a joke teller. "Be happy and don't worry. Life only gets longer, then there's more happiness." He made people feel happy and good. I know how to laugh at life because of him.

I know through my experiences with children that the primary role models in their lives are the people they see daily. I was blessed in that I got to see my grandfather every day. His home was near my grade school. I never ate lunch at the cafeteria; I went to my grandparents' home and loved it! Grandpa was an authority figure but also a man of truth and understanding who made me and others laugh.

The influence of my grandfather upon my life cannot be measured. His thoughts, ideas, and values have made a deep impression on my general outlook on life. There is not a day goes by that I do not think of him or reflect on our relationship. —LINDA L. VAN DYKE

Grandfather loved photography. He had his camera loaded at all times and was ready to capture what was important to him. He took pictures of grandchildren and their friends, of nature, of church functions, of people, and of the simple things in life he cherished. He shared his pictures with everyone.

He had a strong sense of the aesthetic. He could paint, draw, build, and create. He loved music. My grandmother played the organ, and after long days of sign painting, he would sit in his favorite chair and listen and shake his head to the sounds. He couldn't sing a note, but he knew all the words in every verse.

Grandfather loved to fish. He could tell the best fish stories! They were unlike any other fisherman's tales. My grandparents owned a cottage in Minnesota. When I was a child, he expected all of us to spend our summer vacations there. We did. I longed for those wonderful summer days in Minnesota with my cousins as Grandfather taught us all about the beauty of God's world and the peace it can provide. Of course, he had to teach us all to fish also. He would say, "Nature is the art of God."

My grandfather loved the written word. He loved quotations. From my earliest recollection, his shirt pocket always had a small spiral notebook tucked inside. He would write down his thoughts. He taught me early in life that "things and thoughts" were important to write down. Many were his own; others he copied from roadside bulletin boards; many he got from his library of quotation books. He shared this knowledge and all these wonderful words of wisdom and humorous quotes with his many friends.

And for 55 years he painted, at no charge, a bulletin board outside our church. It soon became a ministry for the many people driving by. It also reached the hearts of the congregation on Sunday mornings. It was known as "the wayside pulpit." It became a trademark of our church. On Sunday afternoons, Grandpa would walk to the church with various grandchildren (we had to take turns in accompanying him) to change the sign. We always got a big ice cream cone afterward. We were the first ones to know the message for the next week.

GRANDPA'S FAITH

The most outstanding quality my grandpa had was his ever-present relationship with God. He approached all aspects of life from a spiritual perspective. He led many people to Christ through his consistent testimony and manner of living. He was a spiritually happy man. He believed in the Bible as the force within and behind his life. He taught me that concept at an early age. His life was Christ-centered and church- and family-oriented. I thought he was omnipotent!

Two times in my childhood I saw miraculous healing in my grandfather's life. The first time occurred when he wanted to enclose the front porch so that he

73

and Grandmother could sit out there and enjoy the winter months. But he was overcome by fumes from a gas heater he was using to keep warm while he built the enclosure. I remember receiving the phone call and the quickness of my family getting to his house. All my aunts, uncles, and cousins were there. The preacher was with my grandma, and Grandpa had been taken to the hospital.

Grandpa was not expected to live. We grandchildren were sent to the basement to play. Usually the basement was a beloved place to go—it was where Grandpa kept all his art supplies and where he painted. But though I was just seven years old then, I knew the situation was serious, as did we all, and that day none of us cared to play. My oldest cousin told us to join hands and said that we should all pray. As we prayed, we faced the possibility that we might lose the grandfather we all loved so much. It wasn't time! God had too much for my grandpa yet to do. I doubt that Grandpa's grandchildren ever prayed harder and more fervently than at that moment.

And Grandpa survived! Everyone said it was a miracle. We children knew it for sure, and we knew there was a prayer-hearing God who loved our grandpa as much as we did—and maybe even more. We cousins knew there would be many more ice cream cones with Grandpa when the church bulletin board needed to be changed.

The second miracle occurred when I was 15 years old and was questioning all the "religious stuff"—a far too typical teenager! I was ready to question the principles of Christianity and the weekly attendance at church that was so important in our family. I was "too cool" to be a Christian. I had seen it work in my grandpa's life, but he was an old man and needed it. At least that's how I looked at life then.

But then a large tumor appeared on Grandpa's hand. The tumor was very noticeable—you knew it didn't belong there. The night before the scheduled operation, Grandpa was on the edge of his bed all night long in a constant vigil of prayer. "A prayer in its simplest form is merely a wish turned Godward," he always said.

That night he claimed the promise of healing in James 5, where it says, "The prayer of faith will save the sick, and the Lord will raise him up" (verse 15, NKJV), and he never doubted. In the early morning hours, the physician came to check on Grandpa before taking him in for surgery. Amazingly, the tumor was gone! It was faith in practice. Later I learned that as the family and the doctors anticipated the surgery, Grandpa carried on under the premise of his own anticipation—he would be healed! For years after, he carried the hospital admittance card in his wallet as a testimony to the surgery that never took place. The card yellowed with age, but the message was strong and true each time he pulled it out and told the story.

After Grandpa's miraculous healing, my feelings toward the Christian life changed dramatically, and I was well on my way to a more mature way of looking at things. Grandpa's perspective made the difference. Grandpa's faith impacted me.

As my grandparents' nine grandchildren grew, Grandmother and Grandfather played an important part in their development. Grandfather, in private conversations with each of us, encouraged us to seek a good education, a productive vocation, Christian relationships, marriage, and solid attitudes encompassing love, work, play, appreciation of people, and—most importantly—commitment to God. These attributes were generated in us from our parents, but the basic values they held came from their parents, my grandparents.

As each of us entered college, Grandfather's cartoon letters, quotes, and care packages became treasures. While I attended Vincennes University, the campus post office was so enthralled with his weekly letters to me that they posted them on the bulletin board and the campus newspaper did a feature article on them. What a blessing he was to my life!

Grandpa's drawings were displayed on the wall of my room. Often they had a religious motif. (He sent letters and drawings like that to all of his grandchildren while we were away at college.)

GRANDPA IN EACH OF US

Vocationally, each of Grandpa's grandchildren has a little of him inside each of us. I have the love of writing. While writing my life paper, I didn't need to use notes or an outline. Thinking of him, the memories flowed easily. While reflecting on his influence in my life, and all the things for which I am so grateful, the feelings and the thoughts came directly from my heart. It is easy to write about something good and forceful. My grandpa was that and more.

One cousin is an artist. Three cousins are teachers—one has Grandpa's remarkable sense of humor, one is a Bible teacher, the third is an art teacher. Another is a sign painter (just like Grandpa). One is a policeman who has a strong sense of family. My brother is a sheriff in Florida and is a fishing expert in the Florida Keys and even has his own radio program. (He was the one out of the nine grandchildren who especially loved to go fishing with Grandpa.) Another grandchild was a business major in college and today makes furniture in a workshop filled with Grandpa's tools. And another grandson is a pastor.

Grandpa was wise and trustworthy. He was admired. His life was lived in service to others. In college, I really began to understand this. I was thankful for the honesty and committed life I had seen and experienced in my grandparents and parents. The things I had been taught helped me in the daily challenges of college life. I knew I could trust God and rely on the inner guidance of the Holy Spirit for help.

"Grandma, tell me a story without a book," my little granddaughter used to say, and I immediately knew what she wanted. She wanted to be told again what it was like for her grandma as a child.

Linda Van Dyke's story is like that for me. There is much in it that speaks directly to the subject of the influence of faith. But even more so, it shows what has become an increasingly rare continuity of family as Linda's grandfather and grandmother remained a vital part of all that was going on in the lives of their grandchildren throughout the years.

As grandchildren become young adults and move on into careers, marriage, and parenting. sometimes families drift apart. As grandparents move into retirement and a more leisurely lifestyle, they may find themselves going in different directions, their lives no longer intersecting with their grandchildren's like before. And this, of course, is understandable. But Linda's story reveals key insights into how blessed grandchildren are by the ongoing participation of their grandparents—grandparents who become like wellsprings of stability for children and their families in an unstable world.

And now, as Paul Harvey says, here is "the rest of the story...."

The years progressed. Our grandparents were at all our weddings. Five of us were married in their beloved church—the same church where we'd been dedicated as babies. It made Grandpa proud that all nine of his grandchildren had been baptized in the church and all nine married born-again Christians.

Then we nine became parents. The traditions grew. The heritage had become a reality. Soon there were 16 great-grandchildren. Grandpa was wonderful!

Grandfather loved my sons. My sons loved my grandfather. "If a man is great, he makes others believe in greatness. He makes them incapable of mean ideals and easy satisfaction." It was another of grandfather's sayings.

It wasn't long before the great-grandchildren were doing what we grandchildren had done. They watched Grandpa paint; they laughed at his jokes; they looked at his picture albums; and they sat in church with him eating Lifesavers. They especially loved his quote books.

Grandpa's Unquestioning Love

One of the hardest things I've ever had to do was tell my grandfather I had given birth to a mentally impaired child. I don't know what reaction I expected, but I felt apprehensive—like I was a failure.

I should have known what Grandpa's reaction would be. He held me. He cuddled me like a baby. I cried hard, feeling alone inside. But Grandpa didn't cry. "It's okay, Linda. God gave Danny to all of us." Grandpa loved my Danny. And Danny always came through for Grandpa. Grandpa's love and power reached into the world of the handicapped. Sometimes all it took was a trip to the ice cream store after the bulletin board was changed. Danny felt normal with Grandpa.

As the grandchildren and the great-grandchildren grew, so did the problems in our households, often financial problems. Many of the cousins told me—and I experienced it myself—that Grandpa had a direct line to the power companies. Many times we would go to pay our bills and they would already be paid for the month. He never took the credit, and the power companies were sworn to secrecy.

Grandpa used to tell the story of his and Grandma's experience with the gas company. It was during the Depression and my grandma was cooking potatoes. The gas man came to collect. My grandpa didn't have the money, so the gas was shut off. He told us how humiliating it was to feed his children half-cooked potatoes. He never wanted any of us to experience that kind of shame. When I stood in line to pay my gas bill and found out it was already paid, I always had a picture in my mind of those children eating those awful potatoes!

LIVING THE HERITAGE

In March of 1976, my grandfather lost part of his heart: My grandmother died. He held her hand when she died. It was incredible pain for him, and for the first time in his life, he was thinking only of himself. That was probably the only time that the man had selfish thoughts.

I was expecting my third child at the time of Grandma's death. During her funeral, I had the most incredible feeling of life and death at the same time. As the baby moved inside of me, my body reacted to the stress my heart felt. My grandmother lay stiff but peaceful, her soul in heaven, but my baby was alive and kicking. I will never forget it. It was God's plan of life and death, and I was experiencing it at both levels. I knew my grandfather was still living the heritage, and the protection I felt from his and my grandmother's household was still present in my life. It helped to ease the pain of loss.

It hurt that Grandmother never saw and got to know Jacob. She would have loved him. She liked ornery little boys, and he was certainly that!

"Train up a child in the way he should go, and when he is old he will not depart from it" (Proverbs 22:6, NKJV). That was a verse firmly fixed in Grandpa's mind. Grandpa and Grandma had done that with their children, and they also had the opportunity to remind us, their grandchildren, to do that, and then they helped teach their great-grandchildren the right way to live and grow in the Lord.

After Grandma's death, my husband and I and our three sons made weekly trips to Grandpa's house. I always cooked him dinner. He needed us and we needed him. My grandmother was close in thought and in our hearts, but she was gone. We all took turns taking care of him, but it wasn't the same. For the first time in years, he allowed us to help him. It gave me a sense of self-worth. He had done so much for me.

Grandfather poured his soul into his work. He was 92 years old when he finally died, but his nine-to-five workday continued daily throughout his old age. His finished signs at that time were probably the most beautiful of his long career.

He felt the loss of Grandmother deeply, and it affected his every moment. He hurt. But he taught me the value of a good marriage and how much one partner should mean to the other as they develop a life together. They were married 56 years when she went to be with the Lord. He put 56 roses on her casket.

The most comforting reality of Grandmother's death was the fact that my grandfather believed so strongly in heaven. "The kingdom of heaven is life," he would say. He was also comforted in the realization that my grandma was finally reunited with her baby daughter, Rosemary, who had died from pneumonia at the age of 10 months.

My grandfather selected seeds of nurturing for humanity. He lived in the same house for 72 years. It became an inner-city neighborhood, and soon he was the only white man on the block. But he would never move. This was home. Color of skin meant nothing to him; man was man. I learned to think like that because of Grandpa.

Everyone called him "Grandpa." Little children would visit him in his sign shop, and he always had Lifesavers and Bible tracts for them. He had many friends, young and old.

Grandpa was a simple man. He didn't believe in material things that took his energy or money. He believed in things of the heart. He didn't believe in having things that weren't practical. But one year he bought a beautiful diamond ring with a solid gold band. We were all shocked. The diamond was very big—certainly a departure for Grandfather. But he was very proud of it and wore it for three years until that beautiful October afternoon.

Grandpa's Real Treasures

I remember that October afternoon very well. It was one of those days when the air was crisp, yet the sun made it seem like summer. The trees were beginning to turn. It was just beautiful. My grandfather went to the grocery store that afternoon. When he returned, he took one bag into the house and proceeded to return to the garage to get the second. When he entered the garage, he was grabbed by a big man, knocked down, and hit in the face. The attacker took my grandpa's wallet, $200 in cash, and the ring. He ran down the alley and got away.

Grandpa was 92. What 92-year-old man deserves to be beaten? This was a fellow man? This was humane? Grandpa called me. Matter-of-factly, he said, "Linda, could you come over here? I've been robbed."

I'll never forget the look on his face. He was sitting in his favorite rocking chair on the back porch. His head was bleeding. I've never been so angry! The police and family arrived. He didn't want to go to the hospital. He took me aside and told me what treasures he had lost that were in the wallet. He knew I'd understand. I went up and down that alley looking for pieces of a letter my Aunt Dorothy had written to him 47 years before. He had kept it folded in his wallet. It was a little girl's handwriting and it said, "Daddy, I can't go to Sunday School because I have no shoes."

The other treasure was a picture of my grandma that was taken on their wedding day. The photograph was 64 years old. I never found either one. But nothing was said about losing the ring or looking for it. It wasn't the most important thing taken that day. My grandfather's dignity was. I learned through the message from his heart what was really important in life.

The robber had friends. One night in November, four weeks after the first attack, three men knocked on my grandpa's door and asked to use the phone. Kind, gentle, and understanding as he was, he let them in. They weren't interested in using the phone. They ransacked the house—every room was invaded and torn up. They were looking for my grandpa's treasures that would bring them money. Little did they know his treasures weren't sellable. They held him down. They broke his glasses. They hurt him. The pain was not just physical.

"You must get him out of here. The next time they will kill him." The detective's words were loud and strong. The family knew what had to be done. Grandpa had to leave. There was no other choice. The attackers had succeeded in taking everything from him. "No old people's home, no apartment, no residence, please." Those were his wishes. "I need my family." He was choosing a place to die.

In the space of one week, my grandpa's home was dismantled. After 72 years of memories and special times in his workshop, the house was put up for sale. We all helped. It was death, yet he was alive.

He made lists of everything he owned. He had a good mind. We all received what he wanted us to have. Nobody fought. Nobody argued. Nobody was greedy. It was a lesson in giving—just another of the many lessons we had learned from his life. It was a lesson in love and support for my grandpa and the traditions he taught and by which he had lived. He gave everything away in preparation for his death. He was on his way to heaven and he knew it. And so did we.

A Shoe Box Under His Arm

Grandfather moved to my parents' home. He left his home with a shoe box under his arm. In it were his bank book, his Bible, and a picture of my grandma. Under the other arm was a box of Post Raisin Bran! He ate it every morning, and my mother never bought that kind of cereal. He needed his morning ritual.

He walked away with a smile on his face, saying, "Well, such is life." We were all crying. His smile was on the outside; we knew he was crying on the inside.

"Life is a measure of experiences," I can still hear him say the words, "each one of which makes us bigger, even though sometimes it is hard to realize this. For the world was meant to help us develop character, and we must learn that the setbacks and griefs, which can help us endure life, also enable us to march onward."

The next four months took their toll. He never quite recovered emotionally from the attacks. The attackers were never found, but he prayed for them daily.

I didn't. I couldn't. I hated those men. But I saw Grandpa's plan of action and his willingness to forgive. He lived what he believed and what he was commanded to do by God.

It was Easter of 1985. Everyone was coming to my house for dinner. I expected 26 people. My children love big dinners just as I did as a child. They were busy helping with the decorations and could hardly wait until everyone arrived.

Grandfather gave the most beautiful prayer preceding that dinner that I had ever heard. Grandpa talked to Jesus as if He were sitting at our table eating Easter ham. We were all deeply touched by the power of the prayer. It was his last Easter and the last time my grandfather was ever in my home. Two weeks later he was gone. But he knew it was his time, and the prayer that day was a message to all of us.

We ached. We rejoiced. We wept. Grandfather had spoken so often of seeing our grandmother again. He knew he would get to meet her in heaven. And he knew he would meet God. We were part of his death as we were part of his life. I was able to write part of the memorial service. My cousin, the sign painter, put the last bulletin on the wayside pulpit bulletin board. It said simply: "Good-bye, friends. I'm home now!"

CELEBRATION

The funeral was large—the processional to the cemetery held up traffic for five light changes. Grandfather's funeral was a celebration of life. What a life it had been! I want my life to be like that. I want God to use me. I want to touch other people's lives as Grandpa did. I miss him. He was my best friend. I'm thankful for his love and care for me. My children and grandchildren-yet-to-be have the right to the heritage of family and faith that I have had.

I had to put the anger, the pain, the hurts behind me. I needed to put into practice what Grandpa told me: "The greatest revenge is forgiveness." Profound thought! With God's help, I've been able to do that.

Everyone needs a family. Thank you, Grandpa, for building our family and for being the spiritual leader that you were. I owe you my life. The best tribute I can give to you is to be aware of the blessings your kind of life offers and pass this legacy on to my children and grandchildren.

I'm sure my grandpa is having a wonderful time in heaven. Lots of his friends are there—he made sure they knew how to get there. I'm sure he is loving my grandmother just as he did on earth. And I'm quite sure he's loving that sweet baby named Rosemary. There's one other thing I'm sure of—his crown hardly gets worn because it's so full of jewels and it's just too heavy.

Grandpa, I miss you! Thank you, Grandfather, for the legacy you left.

GRANDPA'S LEGACY

Linda did take to heart what her grandfather said about the need to accept her retarded son. He had said, "Until you learn to respect Danny's struggles, he will make it, but you won't." She never forgot her grandfather's words of wisdom spoken so quietly while sitting with her at the kitchen table.

Because of her grandfather's inspiration, and the love of God that she longed to share with her disabled son and others like him, Linda began a ministry called LUVability. It has grown far beyond First Missionary Church in Niles, Michigan, where through the encouragement and support of her pastor, Dan

Miller, and the congregation, the ministry to the developmentally disabled was begun in 1991.

"Danny learned to grasp the love of God through a variety of methodologies: music, visual arts, story, and drama. Soon he wanted to share his faith with others who have these developmental disabilities," Linda explained. And so the invitations to other churches, institutions, and state homes went out, and the people came, bringing with them those in wheelchairs, unable to walk, some unable to speak, others with Down's syndrome, many unable to communicate in any way other than a smile. "As the word got out, they came in vans transported from group homes by caregivers or staff. It's been amazing to me to see the outreach this ministry has to the caregivers of our disabled friends. Many sit in the back of the church or wherever we are meeting and silently weep as they are ushered into a new realm of understanding by watching their residents or family members express their need for God's love in such a beautiful way.

"Persons with developmental disabilities are often overlooked or even rejected by the church because of who they are, what they look like, and how they think. LUVability says to them, 'You are loved, you have the ability to be loved, and you are part of the body of Christ.' My son told me, 'Mom, I think a lot of people need to learn that people with disabilities don't always get it the way others do. But Mom, we do get it!' And get it they do!

"This is very close to my heart," Linda says, her emotions near the surface as she speaks. "God blessed me with Danny in 1974, although there were many days when I didn't think it was a blessing. Today I delight in being his mother as I see him a strong man of God. He is the foundation and core of LUVability Ministries to the Disabled, and he has brought many Christians to an awareness of servanthood, love, and ministry. God has used our relationship and all the struggles Grandpa told me I would face to bring glory to Him. Never were Grandpa's words heard so strongly than the day Danny 'should' have graduated from high school. It was nothing for Danny, but it was painful, emotional, and full of struggle for me. However, today Danny's life has graduated to beautiful things for God as through our ministry we provide the message to all who are disabled, 'You are loved, you have the ability to be loved, no one loves you like God.' "[1]

7

THAT GIFTED WAY

May you live to see your children's children.
—Psalm 128:6

The headline and a letter in the opinion section of a newspaper caught my attention. The headline read: *Grandparents a Godsend to Boy and Mom*. The letter says it all:

Grandparents! Just where would we be without them? They aren't just the senior citizens we see at Wendy's whom we envy as eligible for an extra discount. They are those knowledgeable people who have a special wisdom to show direction and protection to a child of a single parent.

My son's grandparents offer him a stable environment on a daily basis when I'm at work. He is shown stability, consistency and love. It is a special privilege to be a grandparent. Only they have that gifted way of inspiring the child to love God, because the child feels deep love from them.

One day when my son steps out of my reach and is out on his own I know he'll have the strength to deal with turmoil and crisis because it was instilled in him by his grandparents.[1]

What a great tribute to some very special grandparents!

If becoming a grandmother was only a matter of choice, I should advise every one of you to become one. There is no fun for old people like it!
—HANNAH WHITALL SMITH, 19TH-CENTURY PHILADELPHIA QUAKER

One youngster wrote: "Grandparents are delightful things. They date back to the last century." I don't think he had the twentieth century in mind! The truth is that grandparents seem to be getting younger and younger. Demographers divide the oldest Americans into four age-groups—the sandwich generation (ages 55 to 64), the seasoned citizens (ages 65 to 74), the vintage consumers (ages 75 to 84), and the venerable citizens (ages 85 to 94)—and it is in the last of these groups that we find the most grandparents.

However, not *all* grandparents are in these age-groups. Now many baby boomers have become grandparent boomers. Statistics show that in 1776 only one out of every 50 Americans was over 65 years of age. Today the older adult population is the fastest-growing segment of the United States population, and grandparents are, in a sense, an ever-increasing resource for parents and grandchildren to turn to for the kind of mature wisdom that has accrued to them by virtue of life experiences. However, the older grandparents among us, the World War II veterans, are dropping out of the scene at the rate of more than a thousand a day. Solomon wrote: "The way of life winds upward for the wise, that he may turn away from hell below" (Proverbs 15:24, NKJV).

The newest generation, called the millennial generation, is the largest group to come along since the baby boom. They were born from 1982 on. They offer a challenge to grandparents as we seek to understand their mindset and the culture of today. How can we best do that?

STRATEGIC GRANDPARENTING

In a personal letter from Dale Evans Rogers, written some years ago when I first began collecting information from grandparents, she wrote:

> I believe grandparents should be very strategic in the lives of our grandchildren. We should listen to them before we talk to them. Then we will have earned the right to share our experiences in helping them learn important lessons in life that have helped us. They should know where we stand on the issues they are confronting and on the vital concerns of life, namely,

our relationship to the Lord, to loyalty, truth and kindness to others, and that we have a complete reliance on God in our lives.

If we will give of ourselves to the younger generation, let them know we believe in them, that we really care, we will find our lives satisfying and full of purpose. I want my grandchildren to remember that we served God and that this is so important for them to do. We do that in many ways, by faithfulness in our relationships with family and friends, and also in showing love for and loyalty to our church and to our country.

STEAL-A-GRANDCHILD DAY

I talked to my early-50-something friend Evelyn, who has no grandchildren but has discovered the joy of being a surrogate grandmother. She said, "Today I'm entertaining the 10-year-old daughter of our pastor and his wife, the little girl I told you about." Yes, she had told me about this family, which includes two sons who have an inherited condition that requires almost around-the-clock care from the mother. Evelyn had said she felt concern for the little girl, who understandably doesn't get as much attention as her brothers. "So today is Steal-a-Grandchild Day," she continued. "We're painting tea towels and doing watercolor painting." Meanwhile, in the background, I could hear the animated voice of the little guest. *How wonderful!* I thought and told Evelyn so.

Evelyn has a gifted way about her, and this darling girl is the beneficiary of that. Evelyn is the same age as my oldest daughter, who is a boomer grandmother. Some of us already have great-grandchildren. I find it hard to believe, but I am Great-grandma Helen!

"GREATEST GRANDMOTHERS"

A *Family Circus* cartoon by Bill Keane shows a grandmother with her arms around a little grandchild, and the child is saying, "Megan says she has a great grandmother, but I told her we have the GREATEST grandmother!" We great-grandmothers appreciate such a cartoon.

As members of this "graying of America" population, we possess experience and spiritual power that we could and should be putting to use. Remember Moses? He didn't really start living until he reached 80. What a blessing longevity can be! From the wellspring of our life experiences, we can provide emotional and intellectual support to grandchildren who need stability and continuity as much as, if not more so, than many grandchildren of previous generations. These grandchildren are growing up in a complex, fast-changing world.

We grandparents can be a crucial resource on which today's overstressed families can rely. Sometimes we serve as a sort of cushion protecting these loved ones battered by financial problems, unrelenting schedules, work pressures, job layoffs, and sadly, marital discord and often divorce. Anyone who has enjoyed good grandparenting would view longevity as a distinct blessing. My children have expressed sadness many times that their grandparents are no longer living. Our younger family members want to hang on to their grandpas and grandmas as long as they can, so we need to take charge of our health and do the right things to guard against health problems.

Some grandparents, however, view statistics of longevity as grim. They do not consider a long life to be a blessing, because of the prospect of living on a reduced income, suffering health problems, and for some, having to move to a residential care facility. It's common knowledge that many people in care facilities are neglected by family members. That is so sad. For many years my mother was matron at a Christian home for the aged, and I remember her telling me how happy it made the residents when grandchildren came to see them.

One of my younger friends, Vicki, visits a retirement center and reads to the residents once a week. They love it when she comes. She told me of one lovely grandmother who was able to help her granddaughter and her husband financially by providing the necessary funds for them to adopt a child. The tragedy is that the granddaughter has never brought the child for the grandmother to meet, and the little girl is already six years old. It is hard to believe.

GRANDCHILDREN GIVING TO GRANDPARENTS

The Bible carries warnings about mistreatment of family members. The apostle Paul wrote, "If any provide not for his own, and specially for those of his own house, he hath denied the faith, and is worse than an infidel" (1 Timothy 5:8, KJV). Other versions say such a one is worse than an "unbeliever," but I prefer the word "infidel" in this instance since it seems stronger. The idea is that there is more than one way to provide for one's family members. We can give them love and attention and not just abandon them to a residential care facility. Grandchildren need to be shown how important it is to love and respect one's elders, and if at some point they need to be helped in whatever way, God Himself has shown us that we are to honor, love, and care for them. The apostle Paul stated that proper recognition should be given to those widows who are really in need, but if a widow has children or grandchildren, "these should learn first of all to put their religion into practice by caring for their own family and so repaying their parents and grandparents, for this is pleasing to God" (1 Timothy 5:4). It doesn't hurt for us as grandparents to introduce our children and grandchildren to these biblical admonitions.

My friend Mary Ann Mooney knew from her earliest childhood that to take care of one's grandparents was the biblically right thing to do. "My widowed grandmother came to live with my parents," says Mary Ann, "when they were just a year into their marriage. A maiden aunt also came to live with them. I guess my husband and I followed a family tradition many, many years later when we had my mother—grandmother to our three sons—come to live with us when my father died. We all look back on those six years with Mom in our house as very happy ones."

Mary Ann's mother died about the same time I lost my mother. At the time, Kraig, my young son, in thinking about these two grandmothers, observed, "I guess Mrs. Mooney's mother and Grandma Hattie are—" He paused. Then, having thought over his next statement, he added, "They are shaking hearts in heaven." These dear grandmothers had gone on to their heavenly home, and a little grandson understood this.

THE NEW LONGEVITY

Because we *are* living longer, we have opportunities to kindle the fire of faith not only in our grandchildren but also in our great-grandchildren and even—for some us—in our great-great-grandchildren. How important for us to see this as the wonderful opportunity it is to be on the cutting edge of what's happening in our world today!

At whatever point in life this book finds you, the reality is that today we aren't aging in the same way our grandparents and parents did. We're more active and health conscious. We have different attitudes about food. We are more informed about what to do and what not to do to increase our chances of healthy longevity.

In this regard, I want to inform you about a book by my friend Judy Lindberg McFarland, entitled *Aging Without Growing Old* (Western Front, Ltd., 2000). The book is full of essential information for people of all ages who seek a lifetime of good health. One of the most important investments any of us can make is the investment in our own health, and regardless of the state of your health now, it's never too late to makes changes and take charge of your health. Judy and her husband, Don, have four married children and 12 of the healthiest, most beautiful grandchildren imaginable. They are a tribute to the philosophy that Judy espouses. Judy can also be seen frequently on the *700 Club* and *TBN*.

Grandparenting Beyond Bloodlines

Many seniors are serving as Sunday school teachers and participating in summer Vacation Bible School programs. My own mother served the Lord faithfully year after year in this way. Little children and young people by the dozens adored their "Grandma Hattie." At her memorial service, her pastor said in an emotion-filled voice, " 'Grandma Hattie' was my Sunday school teacher when I was a boy in Iowa. She had a tremendous influence on my life and my decision to enter the ministry."

One of the finest ways to preserve a good quality of life after embarking on the so-called retirement age is to serve others. I saw this kind of self-giving love extended by the seniors in the First Baptist Church of Sunnyvale, California, where my husband served as associate pastor for six years. There were many widows in the church, and I'm sure their loving the young people in the church was not only filling a deep need for the children, it was reciprocal; these lovely ladies were being loved in return. Many, if not most, of them knew a great deal about loneliness.

Many community programs welcome senior members, and you are well advised to look in the yellow pages or to call your local chamber of commerce and learn how you can offer your services. Surrogate grandparenting, or foster grandparenting (it goes by different names), is always appreciated by lonely, neglected children who desperately need care, love, and attention.

IT'S OFTEN THE LITTLE THINGS THAT COUNT THE MOST

Dale Evans Rogers told me about her Grandfather Wood, who read the Bible at bedtime around the fire, sharing a piece of fruit with his grandchildren and praying nightly for them. He was kindling a faith fire. She also remembered her Great-grandfather Wood, from Italy, Texas, who lost his eyesight for a while. "He would walk down the middle of the road on his way to prayer meeting each Wednesday night," Dale recalled. "He received his second eyesight and lived to be 94."

She remembered her Grandmother Wood also, churning the milk on the screened-in porch, singing the old hymns, or reading her *Baptist Standard* and her Bible. "I was seven," she wrote. The gifted way of these dear grandparents lived on in Dale's heart even when she herself was a grandparent and great-grandparent.

I told Dale that I remembered my Grandpa Brunsting sharing fruit with me also before bedtime when my mother, sister, and I lived with him for a time following the death of our grandmother. Grandpa insisted on reading the Bible in the Dutch language, and his prayers (also in Dutch) were long and drawn out. He wasn't prone to showing much affection. "Pa," Mother would say, "you should read the Bible and pray in English so Dorothy and Helen would understand."

"No," he would gruffly respond, "this way they will learn to understand and speak Dutch." Did I? The answer, I assure you, is no. But I can still hear the sound of his voice reading and praying. Even though I couldn't understand much of what he was saying, I knew it was a good thing he was doing. And I did like it when he shared his apple. Grandpa was kindling a flame too and, in his own way, showing love.

Our memories are colored by these faith-filled, faithful old grandparents who lived their lives in such a way as to inspire faith in their grandchildren. Simple things, but cherished memories. It's the little things that often count the most. I remember my grandpa's pink peppermints doled out (none too generously) among his many grandchildren on Sunday afternoons when we all gathered at his big Iowa home after church. You could make a pink peppermint last a long time, and we used to say, "See, I still have mine," as we'd stick out our pink tongues.

What will today's grandchildren remember? Grandpa and Grandma stepping off the jet at Christmastime and spending fun-filled days at their house? Grandpa and Grandma watching one of the new Christian videos with them? Grandpa and Grandma praying with them? Grandpa and Grandma curling up with them in front of the fire and reading one of their favorite Bible story books? Mary Ann Mooney told me that when her first grandson was born, her son Jon asked for the worn Catherine Vos Bible story book that had been read to him as a little boy. "He read it to his two children, and I had the privilege of praying with our grandson Josh to receive Christ when he was four and stayed all night with us."

Many people told me they passed on favorite storybooks to their grandchildren, perhaps reminding them, "Your mother loved these stories when she was little." For many years, whenever I needed to give someone a baby gift, I went to the local

Christian bookstore for a copy of *The Bible in Pictures for Little Eyes*—a book my own children had been raised on, written by Dr. Kenneth Taylor, himself the father of 10 (and as the years progressed, becoming the grandfather of 27). I divvied up my children's favorite books (of which there were many, since we were in the Christian bookstore business) as they started presenting us with grandchildren. It was such fun! Some of those books had teeth marks—reminders of teething days. Others had pictures colored with crayon that had been added.

One grandmother wrote me, saying, "I've raised my kids and done my job. Now it's their turn, and I'll live my own life. I'll see them if I'm needed or invited, but none of this free baby-sitting service for me."

I read somewhere about a young mother, saddened because her parents didn't want to be "bothered" with seeing the grandchildren. She explained how her parents expected her family to take care of their pets when they went out of town, but that they wouldn't drop in to see the children, or even suggest her husband and she drop them off while they went to dinner for a few hours. Apparently, baby-sitting "wasn't their thing."

Don't such grandparents realize what they are missing? Contrast that kind of attitude to the dozens of letters I received from grandparents telling how much they love baby-sitting.

It's just another opportunity to play games, work puzzles, throw the Frisbee, and let the grandkids help with cooking and baking. Kids love grating carrots, breaking eggs into a batch of cookie [dough]—things like that. When they stay overnight, it's really special. At bedtime we sing Sunday school songs, play tapes, read Bible stories, and pray. Everything we do I consider an opportunity to share Jesus' love with them. We are building memories.

Alice Guffee, a grandmother from Parker, Texas, wrote:

We love to garden and we involve our grandchildren in this. I plant herb gardens that draw butterflies, and I've taught them what to plant (parsley and dill) so the butterflies can lay their eggs, and then we watch the caterpillars grow and complete the cycle to butterflies again. We also identify different plant materials. Our granddaughter Andrea got her grandfather to help her do a project of plant identification for school. They went out into the neighborhood and visited some garden centers.

American musical theater is also something we have taken them to see. *Joseph and the Amazing Technicolor Dreamcoat* they especially liked.

I would love to be one of this couple's grandchildren! Which sort of grandparent would you want to have?

8

INTERCESSORS: THE RIGHTEOUS FAITHFUL

Your faithfulness continues
through all generations.
—PSALM 119:90a

Over and over again, when conducting my research for this book, I read or heard the refrain "Grandma (or Grandpa) was an intercessor." There was consistent emphasis on the role prayer played in the lives of these faith-filled grandparents.

The poem that follows expressed the idea of intercession so beautifully, I've chosen to include it here at the outset. It is taken from Amy Carmichael's book *Toward Jerusalem*. It's titled, "For Our Children":

Father, hear us, we are praying,
Hear the words our hearts are saying,
We are praying for our children.

Keep them from the powers of evil,
From the secret, hidden peril,
From the whirlpool that would suck them,
From the treacherous quicksand, pluck them.

From the worldling's hollow gladness,
From the sting of faithless sadness,
Holy Father, save our children.

Through life's troubled waters steer them,
Through life's bitter battle cheer them,
Father, Father, be Thou near them.
Read the language of our longing,
Read the wordless pleadings thronging,
Holy Father, for our children.

And wherever they may bide,
Lead them Home at eventide.

Bonnie Campbell, a gifted young musician, composed a work entitled "Grand Portraits in Four Movements" as a musical tribute to her grandparents. Each movement was dedicated to one of them. Bonnie and her parents, Dr. Everett and Louise Campbell, shared the following information with me.

Bonnie began by pointing to the words of Coleman Barnes:

Oh, the rhythm of life has a powerful beat,
Puts a tingle in your fingers
and a tingle in your feet,
Rhythm on the inside, rhythm on the street,
Oh, the rhythm of life has a powerful beat.

"All life is rhythmic," Bonnie wrote. "Rhythm is bound up in the essence of life. Our own personal rhythm harks back to our predecessors," she explained, "—ancestors who have, in part, determined the shape of our rhythm in its foundations." She speaks of a deeper level of meaning to her own life that is a result of the "life rhythm of four people who have shaped the foundation of my life, my grandparents."

Referring to this rhythm of life, Bonnie says, "There is much dancing and teaching for us to do too. As we all move together, seeking after the knowledge of life, it is my belief that we, humankind, will find branches of knowledge even more interrelated and unified. And we will see its vast polyrhythmic structure. My grandparents were all people of vision. They taught me by their example that the rhythm of life is simple and should not be fought but followed."

Bonnie knew about following in the footsteps of her grandparents, godly men and women of faith. In particular, the legacy of her paternal grandmother made an enormous impact on her thinking. She wrote:

Grandma was an amazing woman. I have never seen anyone who possessed a greater spirit of gentle kindness. She took everything in stride.... Nothing fazed her. I think that she had it all right from the very beginning.

Praying was always a big part of Grandma's life. I am sure that her spirit was largely a result of it. I know that she used to pray for me, and sometimes I feel that her prayers on my behalf are still being answered, even after her death.

PRAYER IS HARD WORK

Dozens of grandparents told me that prayer is hard work, especially those who are grandparenting by long distance. The restrictions this imposed on their ability to baby-sit, invite grandchildren over for Sunday dinner, or participate in birthdays and holidays were all recurring themes. But one thing all these grandparents mentioned was that they could pray for their grandchildren.

Intercessory prayer! It is always a joy and a privilege to receive a call or an e-mail from a grandchild requesting prayer. "Pray for our animals," one will say, and he will proceed to elaborate on Scooter's ear infection or Calli's limp. Trivial? Not at all! Pets are a big part of our grandchildren's lives, and they know that nothing is too big or seemingly too small for Grampa and Gramma to pray about—and that God is interested too.

When everything in us yearns to participate in the lives of these grandsons and granddaughters, we can cry out to God in intercessory prayer. When we long for hugs and kisses, and we sense they may be longing for that from us, we can send telegram prayers upward: *Dear Father, let the grandchildren sense our love and feel secure in the knowledge that we pray for them.* And then we can do an "inventory assessment," if you will, of what's going on in their lives, as we intercede on their behalf.

Praying for the ongoing inspiration, inner guidance, and spiritual help these grandchildren need is a daily discipline, but adding to those prayers the specifics about what's going on in their lives demands that we stay in touch with them. Praying about the details keeps us on our toes so that we will know what to pray about, what their needs, hopes, dreams, frustrations, anxieties, fears, concerns, joys, and expectations actually are. Their knowing that we do this kind of praying is a reminder *to them* to keep in touch. The e-mails keep coming; I love receiving them. Now and then there will be a phone call. We certainly never run out of things to intercede about for them. It helps to keep a prayer list—the inventory assessment idea. It's great when you can cross off a specific prayer request and even show it to the grandchild for whom you were praying something special. You bet they are impressed—impressed with God! Perhaps your grandchild, like Bonnie Campbell, will someday say of you that your prayers on behalf of her or him are still being answered.

Evelyn Christenson, in her book *What Happens When We Pray for Our Families,* says that prayer acknowledges God as Director of our families. I have always told my family that after we pray, we trust God for direction and answers and do what I call "the near-at-hand things" to bring order and stability into our lives. Evelyn calls it "putting feet to our prayers." We trust and obey and, as best we can, we discern what we need to say, do, or be. Evelyn points out that prayer is not in place of action; it is getting the wisdom and power for that action.

THE EXAMPLE

Gigi Graham Tchividjian, the firstborn of Billy and Ruth Graham's five children and a mother of seven herself, makes mention of her grandparents in her charming book *Sincerely.* She tells of staying overnight at the home of her maternal grandparents and of tiptoeing down the steps in the morning to spy on her grandfather as he prayed. "Yes, he was there as he was every morning, on his knees in front of the big rocking chair. I stood watching him until LaoNaing [Chinese for *Grandmother*] called us to breakfast. He got up slowly, rubbing his eyes before he replaced his glasses, his forehead still red and creased from the impact of his folded hands. He saw me and smiled. Giving me a warm hug and a big kiss, we went into the kitchen together."

Gigi continued, "I knew that this active surgeon, church layman, writer, former missionary to China, and family man had been up long before dawn, spending time with the Lord. He had an extensive prayer list, and I felt warm and secure, knowing he had already prayed for me. Now he was refreshed and eager to meet the rest of his busy day."

Gigi says her grandfather never disappointed her as a man or as a Christian. "Until the day he died, he set an example of practical, balanced, fun-loving, disciplined, godly living."

Certainly these grandparents exemplified 1 Timothy 4:12:

"Be an example to the believers in word, in conduct, in love, in spirit, in faith, in purity" (NKJV).

I found it interesting that both Bonnie Campbell and Gigi spoke of their grandparents as being examples. This is worth thinking about, grandparents. We should ask ourselves: *Am I the right kind of example to my grandchildren? Could they say that about me?*

CALLED TO A MINISTRY OF PRAYER, REJOICING, AND THANKSGIVING

A writer friend told me she felt called to "a ministry of prayer, rejoicing, and thanksgiving" for her grandchildren. "Pray without ceasing" (1 Thessalonians 5:17, KJV) should be a reality in the lives of grandparents. What does that mean? It means to have an *attitude* of prayer, regularly and constantly. It doesn't depend on posture or place. It doesn't mean the abandonment of tasks and duties and times of rest. But the command should not be minimized either. It means life should be lived in a continual spirit of prayer—God in our thoughts always. Beneath the stream of thought and activities there should flow the deep current of unconscious communion with God and the sense of His presence. It's a current that rises to conscious petition and prayer.

T. W. Wilson and Billy Graham enjoyed a friendship that had its beginnings when they were both in their teens, according to Mary Helen Wilson. Understandably, the memories T. W.'s loved ones carry with them are a legacy of love, a meaningful and beautiful heritage. In watching the video of the memorial service for T. W. Wilson, I was deeply moved when an in-law, Byron Bledsoe, said what he noticed about the grandfather's prayers. Here's how he expressed it at the memorial service:

I had the privilege of calling him Granddad Wilson, because I married his first granddaughter. There are many ways that he impacted my life, but I especially remember his prayers. Now, I grew up in church and I've heard a lot of prayers, but I'd never heard anything like what I heard when he prayed.

Over the period of years, as I got to know him better and was welcomed into the family, there was something that might seem insignificant about the way he prayed, but really it was very significant. It was the way, most of the time, he would begin. Because so much of the time, when he began praying, he didn't say, "God ..." or "Father ..." He began with the word "And ..." In fact, often he would say, "And now, our Father ..." And it just reminded me, as I thought about his life and I learned so much from him, that this was a man that when you heard him pray, you weren't just listening to him for the first time he talked to God that day. You were stepping into a conversation that was continual and ongoing all the time because he was a man who walked in prayer and understood prayer and was close to his heavenly Father.

When we got word about what had happened [his death], I told Angie, "I remember Robert Louis Stevenson once wrote, 'Sooner or later we all sit down to a banquet of consequences.'" I believe that Granddad Wilson is at a banquet of consequences—the consequences of a life of faith and a life of prayer, a man who was close to his Lord.

I can honestly say, as not only a family member, but as a younger preacher, that I am closer to Christ today because of Granddad Wilson.[1]

Statistics say there are 60 million grandparents in America. This represents a lot of people power. How many of those could be a strong influence for change through prayer? We need to work at it, and one of the best places to begin is with our grandchildren. Intercessory prayer can be the starting point.

INSOMNIA AS PRAYER AID

Insomnia is a recurring problem for some grandparents. Some told me they have learned to turn waking night hours into prayer time. One referred to these hours as "uninterrupted quality time for intercession." I know that in the last months of my husband's life, in particular, he had a lot of discomfort that interrupted his sleep. I would find him praying, his prayer list in front of him. And oh, how he prayed for his grandchildren!

Trying times demand that we, as prayer intercessors, be vigilant and faithful. We are living in a godless society that requires godly grandparenting as never before. Keeping a pen and a prayer notebook near the bed is an aid when sleep eludes us. Writing down these prayer needs helps to clarify what may be going on in the life of a loved one. It helps to gain the right perspective sometimes when you see something in black and white. Some of us keep a running prayer list on our computers.

Many grandparents carry heavy burdens—we know we are to cast them on the Lord, but we are very human, and God knows all about that too. The breakup of families impacts grandparents in some heartbreaking ways. The stress our children and grandchildren encounter in their upward striving to attain educational goals, and in career pursuits and business decisions, is real. Spike and Darnell White *(I Need You),* in passing on tips about being friends with your grandkids, say that grandparental prayer is not the whole solution, but it sure does provide a lot of answers and inspiration. "Besides, when praying for them we can't be accused of 'interfering' in the kids' lives, because only God knows. A child who is prayed for 365 days a year, for however many years of life, is bound to be on God's 'TO DO' list. That's a lot of praying by the time that grandchild is grown."

My grandchildren have known from the time they were able to understand such things that Grandma does a lot of "telegram praying." I tell them, "Whenever Grandma is concerned about you, she just turns that concern into a telegram prayer. 'Help!' I say. 'Help, dear God, Jesse needs your help!'" (Or whichever grandchild sent a specific request my way.) And I have taught them to do the same thing. "You can send your own telegram prayers. God is always on the receiving end. There is something that is faster than a fax, an e-mail, or a phone call—it's the direct connection we have to a prayer-hearing and a prayer-answering heavenly Father."

A Mother's and Grandmother's Influence in Prayer

I learned something some years ago from Morrow Graham, Billy Graham's mother, when I had the privilege of spending time with her in their Charlotte, North Carolina, family home. She spoke of the concern she had for Billy when he was in high school and his grades were suffering. The teacher finally told her that Billy might not make the grade. "Oh no, that can't be," she replied. "I felt like I had just been chopped through the heart." Mrs. Graham confided, "I prayed, *O Lord, that can't be true. You'll just have to do something for my boy.*" She finished that simple prayer by saying, *Lord, You are preparing Billy for something, and whatever it is, Lord, it's Your problem.*

Mrs. Graham's account of that episode in Billy's life ended like this: "You know, I left that problem with the Lord, and by the end of the school year, when he was 17, he had made the grades to graduate. It was surely a test for me as his mother, but God saw him through."

God saw him through. What a lesson I learned from Mrs. Graham, that I can safely leave my children's and grandchildren's problems with the Lord, and He will see them through. This is the access we have been given to secure God's help on behalf of our grandchildren.

Mrs. Graham told me she also prayed unceasingly for her other children, for her 12 grandchildren, and for her great-grandchildren.

When Billy began his preaching ministry, back in his Florida Bible Institute days, he was heard to say, "The road to hell is blocked with many interferences. If you go to hell, it will be your own deliberate choice, as God is doing His best to keep you out of there." Speaking on the theme of "God's Blockade," young Billy went on to explain: "Before a person can sink there, he must climb over the Bible, a mother's influence in prayer, the Holy Spirit, the mountain of reason, and the cross of Christ."

"A mother's influence in prayer"—the words stand out. As I concluded my interview with Mrs. Graham those long years ago, in her shy, unassuming way, she commented, "We try. As mothers, we try. Yet there is so much of weakness and failure in our own lives, we just wonder how God overlooks all of this and brings good out of evil. We had such long hours and hard work, but we surely did read the Bible and pray."

That made the difference.

Mrs. Graham is no longer living, but her memory and the rich legacy of her faith-filled life endures. She would never admit to being a great mother behind a great son—or even a great grandmother behind great grandchildren—but she did confirm that she had a great God, one who lavishes blessings unto one's children and children's children.

Prayer should be the spontaneous lifestyle of every Christian family especially today because the family as the world has known it for centuries is disintegrating before our eyes. —EVELYN CHRISTENSON IN
WHAT HAPPENS WHEN WE PRAY FOR OUR FAMILIES

Jennifer, a 50-year-old boomer grandmother, recalled staying with her grandmother overnight from time to time and being able to see her from the bedroom where she slept.

I would watch her in the room across the hall and see her place her hands over her face and pray. When she opened her eyes, I didn't want her to know I had been watching her from the other room. But oh, that made such a lasting impression on me!

Today I have five grandchildren of my own, and I've made sure they know that I pray for each of them by name each day and that they can let me know what they want me to pray about for them. I've also taught them, of course, that they must go to God themselves and talk to Him. Moreover, they've been taught that we don't just pray to God expecting handouts, but that we must also thank and praise Him for being our heavenly Father.

Now a widow, Jennifer was a Wycliffe missionary with her husband, who was a Bible translator in a Peruvian jungle for many years. She spoke of her parents devotedly praying for them and their children every day, and of how these parents sacrificially gave to their family's support.

I would often remind our children that they had grandparents in the States who faithfully prayed for them. But I know from firsthand experience that the grandparent-grandchild relationship can suffer when there is prolonged separation. To help create faith in grandchildren requires a two-way loving relationship, and prayer is the bond that maintains that relationship though separated by distance. Then if the grandparents communicate with their grandchildren, especially through writing letters, and they themselves remind the grandchildren that they pray for them without ceasing, even as the Bible instructs, this imprints into the grandchild's thinking. I, myself, am living proof that God answers a grandmother's prayers.

[My father's mother] died when my father was 21 after living a very hard life with many children, poverty, and an alcoholic husband. Her dying words were that my father, her 13th and last child, might turn to the Lord. (He was already showing signs of alcoholism.) When I, 25 years later, came home with my testimony of accepting Christ into my life, I expected it would anger my father. But he said not a word and shortly thereafter became a believer. I was able to speak to him about the Lord and God's love and faithfulness. Then he told me that he recognized what God was doing in my life as the answer to his mother's prayers. Later, when I married and gave birth to a daughter, I named her Ellen for that grandmother whose prayers God answered after she died. I treasure the memory of her faithfulness, which others have told me about, telling me that she prayed also for her grandchildren yet unborn.

Be vigilant in prayers for your children and grandchildren, those living and those yet to be. Not all prayers are answered at 10:20 in the morning two days after they are prayed. Sometimes those prayers are answered years later as a result of our grandchildren's faith.

A SOCIETY OF FOUR-LETTER WORDS

We are living in what has rightly been described as a post-Christian society. The late Leonard LeSourd (the late Catherine Marshall's husband) said that we are living in a four-letter world—a world that can be described with words like *evil, guns, kill, fear, poor, sick, worn, vile*. We hear a lot about four-letter-word combinations in radio and television news reports and in the print media: *hate* crimes, date *rape, drug* deals. You can think of other word combinations, I'm sure. But there is another four-letter word that is one parents and grandparents alike can cling to. It is a word that speaks of refuge and hope in this bewildering world—it is the word *pray*. Grandparents are so very good at this. We know how to pray!

Which surely leads to a greater appreciation of the role of strong, right relationships, particularly that of family, and the need to authenticate the gospel message by our lives. Ours is such a significant role—if our grandchildren turn their backs on their heritage of faith, they will be left to face the disappointments and crises of life by themselves, and that means they are hopelessly outmatched.

Some grandchildren don't remember having fun times with

their grandparents, but they do recall their prayers. One woman wrote:

> My maternal grandfather had a profound influence on my faith, but he was a very serious man. I don't remember him for any "fun" I ever had with him. But he was godly, patient, kind, concerned. He had great respect for God's Word. I especially remember his prayers and testimonies in church and his reading the Bible and praying before anyone could leave the table at mealtime. I remember him coming to our house and discussing spiritual matters and praying with my mother.

Although he left the impression of being an austere man, this woman harbors no ill feelings for her grandfather. Thankfully, she recognized that even though he didn't take time to have fun with her, he was a serious-minded, godly man whom she should respect. Perhaps he could have been more lighthearted, but seriousness was in his nature, and if we ourselves have that tendency, we might want to remember that sour saints aren't any more spiritual than those who can smile, laugh, and express a joy-filled attitude.

A HANNAH

A woman from New York state (who was referred to me by mutual friends who called her "an exemplary grandmother in every way") wrote:

I remember my grandmother as being a woman of prayer. She lived with us part of the time, and I was always impressed with the length of her prayers each night before she retired. She prayed like Hannah—her lips were moving, but you couldn't hear her. I wondered if I could ever become a pray-er as she was. She left me with the impression, by her life and influence, that she was a godly woman.

This same woman remembers her great-grandmother as being a kind and considerate woman who was also what she called "a pray-er." That legacy was handed down to her, and it's no wonder that her friends think of her as being "an exemplary woman of prayer."

9

THE SILENT SAVIORS

The prayer of a righteous man is powerful and effective.
—JAMES 5:16b

A nurse friend of mine, who specialized in drug and alcohol rehabilitation at a veteran's hospital for 14 years, now works in a state-run correctional facility. She told me that, almost without exception, patients and inmates will tell you that the only positive role models they've had in their lives have been grandparents. Is that startling or what?

A large number of grandparents told me they consider their most important role as being a prayerful counselor to their grandchildren. "Available, always praying for them, and having to counsel them," one grandmother said.

It is next to impossible to separate the prayers of grandparents from what is included in this chapter—they are so deeply entwined. As grandparents, we get through because we are prayers. How good it is to remember this. We can *know* that God has heard. Prayer. That's our job, to pray without ceasing and to let our loved ones know that we are always available to them.

Vine's *Expository Dictionary of New Testament Words* provides a definition of "effectual," and it adds a dimension to James 5:16 we may not have considered before. The dictionary say that "effectual" refers to "the effect produced in the praying person, bringing him into line with the will of God." Praying "in the will of God" means being conformed to the will of God as we pray. Evelyn Christenson emphasizes that the effectual pray-er is a person who is completely committed to God's will for answers and not to his own will. Sometimes that means letting go so completely that we literally have to stand back and take a hands-off stance. Not easy!

Be forewarned: The material in this chapter covers some difficult territory. Not all of these problems have easy answers. But our true source of hope is always available.

AN UNSTABLE WORLD

For some grandparents, providing counseling is being available when a new mother calls, explains her baby's problem, and asks, "Grandma, what should I do now?" We especially love it when a grandchild calls or sends an e-mail asking for our prayers.

But for some grandparents, there are gigantic hurdles to be faced in seeking to be a part of their grandchildren's lives. For them, counseling may come in the form of helping a grandchild who has gotten in trouble with the law. And from going to traffic court with the grandchild to visiting the grandchild on death row, grandparents have been there.

The words from James 5:16 burn a hole in my heart, for it is the power of prayer that needs to be unleashed against the evils that seek to destroy our grandchildren and great-grandchildren. The old familiar King James Version says, "The effectual fervent prayer of a righteous man availeth much." When Evelyn Christenson points to the disintegration of today's families, she says the answer is a lifestyle of spontaneous prayer.

And in Romans 8:

> The Spirit also helps our weakness; for we do not know how to pray as we should, but the Spirit Himself intercedes for us with groanings too deep for words; and He who searches the hearts knows what the mind of the Spirit is, because He intercedes for the saints according to the will of God. (vv. 26-27, NASB)

Evelyn says that when she is uncertain how to pray about something that concerns a loved one, she just prays, "O Holy Spirit, I don't know how or what to pray for Kathy [or whomever]. Please take my 'not knowing how to pray as I ought' to the Father according to His will."[1]

There are situations where divorce has stolen grandchildren and legal challenges intrude. Or there may be drug or alcohol addictions. Or maybe the problem is wife or child abuse. This is serious stuff that turns a grandparent's hair gray really fast. One young grandmother sent an e-mail requesting prayer because her daughter was going through her third divorce and the daughter's three children were being separated. One grandfather was coming to the rescue. As Jay Kesler says, "Today's youth are facing more serious challenges than previous generations. Today's drugs aren't cornsilks smoked behind the barn. And drugs and pornography aren't things they outgrow. It isn't a situation where everybody does a little bit, realizes it was foolish and goes on. Some of these things can't be moved on from."[2]

Some of the drug-related problems grandparents are encountering have to do not just with teenage grandchildren but with their own children, the parents of their grandchildren. Or the problem may be with the grandchildren who become parents at a very young age, turning the grandparents into great-grandparents. It can become very convoluted. But for children of drug-ridden parents, there's no love like that of a grandparent or great-grandparent. This dual role has become all too common in families torn apart by drug abuse.

I have read story after heartrending story showing grandparents and great-grandparents bearing drug's devastating burden. Such grandparents have had to step out from behind their shame to secure legal, financial, and emotional help, not to mention Pampers, formula, and cribs. Some of the babies born to drug-addicted mothers are themselves addicted or later will show signs of severe neglect and even abuse. Fortunately, many agencies across the country that deal with the multifaceted problem do recognize that it is the grandmothers, in particular, who are the best people to turn to for help. Yet even so, it is difficult for grandparents to gain unchallenged permanent custody or even temporary financial help.

THE WAR ON THE FUTURE OF GRANDCHILDREN

"There's no war on drugs," one grandmother said; "it's a war on the future of our grandchildren." Grandparents who enter the battle to try and get custody of grandchildren encounter severe problems. They have had to watch as their grown children sank into a world of drugs, taking the children—their grandchildren —with them into squalor, corruption, and the seedy lifestyle and underworld of physical and emotional violence.

Many of these grandparents are retired or nearing retirement age. Nearly 4 million American children under the age of 18 are being raised in a grandparent's home. A lot of these elders are living on fixed incomes. Now they are faced with the needs of their grandchildren—they must be fed, clothed, educated. To whom do the grandparents turn for help? The overworked welfare and social services systems often want to reunite children with parents, regardless of how much grandparents have done for them.

The scenario goes something like this: The children's mother holds on to her children long enough to get food stamps and welfare money, and then the money goes for drugs, not for apartment rent. She may even sell their food stamps to get money for drugs. Then the mother finally turns the children over to their grandmother. Eviction may follow unless someone forks over the rent. Either that or the addicted mother ends up on the street— or who knows where! She may end up in jail, where she might be kept for a while, but usually only briefly.

FALLING BETWEEN BUREAUCRATIC CRACKS

Enter Children's Protective Services that says the children must be sent where they will be cared for. What about Grandma? Grandmothers fall between the bureaucratic cracks. If Grandma does succeed in getting the children, she isn't compensated nearly enough for what she gives the children. Such monies are preferentially allotted to foster families or an agency, and they will receive four or more times as much as a grandparent. Under the law, strangers who take in foster children get more money, clothing allowances, counseling, and health benefits than relatives taking care of their own. If grandparents take them in and can't make it financially, the children can be taken from them and given up as wards of the state.

STEPPING IN TO RESCUE GRANDCHILDREN

In December 1991, *U.S. News & World Report* did a front-page story entitled "Grandparents: The Silent Saviors." The photo of the grandmother hugging her granddaughter, with another forlorn-looking granddaughter leaning against a tattered door frame, etched itself into my thinking. As I write this, I'm looking at the magazine again. It talks about the millions of grandparents who have stepped into the breach to rescue children from faltering families, drugs, abuse, and violent crime—the "silent saviors." Since 1991, hundreds of such stories have been uncovered. But this particular issue really got to me. The story explains that nothing can ease the unique burdens these grandparents bear. Furthermore, many of them are racked by shame and guilt at the fact that their own children have failed as parents—and many blame themselves. I know this to be true because, for a book I wrote entitled *You Never Stop Being a Parent,* I sent out questionnaires and received a large response, in which many parents said they found it difficult to get away from their guilt.

The magazine article further explained that in order to provide safe and loving homes to their grandchildren, some grandparents must emotionally abandon their own abusive or drug-addicted children. The grandchildren themselves are not only terribly needy in every physical way, but they are also emotionally damaged and very angry. "There is not a town in America untouched by this version of the extended family," the story emphasized. It is believed that there are at least 3.9 million custodial grandparents in the United States.

Without much effort, I can think of numerous families we have met who have borne this kind of heartache, some for decades. Drugs, crime, and financial and emotional distress have split families apart. When my husband was an associate pastor at two churches—one in the Midwest, another in northern California—he would come home visibly shaken by some of the problems he encountered. Court dockets are overcrowded with custody cases involving children under 18. Grandparents have had to become parents again. Many have had grandchildren stolen from them through dying of AIDS. Cocaine addiction has also stolen not only children but grandchildren. There are stories of nine-year-old girls with gonorrhea, having been repeatedly raped by the addicted mother's boyfriends. Parents have had to come to terms with their heartache as they have entered legal battles to gain custody of precious grandchildren. Some stories have been featured on television programs such as *Oprah*. It is no exaggeration to say that the worst and most lasting wounds are the emotional ones, often requiring much counseling. But sometimes the children themselves show a remarkable resiliency, especially when they have experienced the nurturing of a loving and caring grandmother.

The *U.S. News & World Report* article reported that if grandparents who have become parents again could wave a magic wand, at the top of their wish list would be a liberalization of the laws regulating child custody in these difficult cases where the child's natural parents are unfit to care for the child. Parental rights are given too much weight in clear-cut cases when custody should be changed.

Not only does drug addiction invade families and tear them apart, but also violent crime can turn the world upside down in every way for those who are victims and survivors. Imagine how you would feel if your daughter was murdered, the murder went unsolved, your grandchildren were turned over to the father, and he made it difficult for you to gain access to your grandchildren.

Then there is the burden of poverty that grandparents face when struggling to feed extra mouths and put shoes and clothes on little bodies when they are granted custody. The toll of age and finances is exacting.

It is an all-consuming role such grandparents have chosen to take. Elaine Shelton, a West Palm Beach, Florida, grandmother is a case in point. Since 1996, she has been raising her nine-year-old grandson. Her heart goes out to grandparents, and she is fond of saying, "We're off our rockers." There's a double meaning to her comment, of course, but it does strike at the need for sanity in the role of grandparenting (and sometimes great-grandparenting). In fact, she has started work on a Web site to help others like herself.[3] Her faith is what keeps her going.

WHEN DIVORCE STEALS YOUR GRANDCHILDREN

More heartaches occur when divorce steals grandchildren and the custodial parent refuses to allow the grandparents to see their grandchildren. Nowadays it isn't rare for grandparents to sue for such visitation rights when an ex-daughter-in-law or ex-son-in-law with children no longer keeps in touch or deliberately bans visitation. But litigation is costly and takes time, and even if a court grants grandparents visitation rights, the underlying problems that gave rise to the breakdown in family relations may continue, and a longed-for relationship with one's grandchildren may be strained.

It is wise to seek an attorney if you have problems or questions about grandparents' rights. But as Marianne Walters, director of the Family Therapy Practice Center in Washington, D.C., said, "Once you have to go to court to assert your rights as a grandparent, you've already lost something precious."[4] Nevertheless, if it becomes necessary for you to seek legal counsel, your local library's reference department should be able to provide information on family law and procedures. You are well advised to ask yourself some questions: *Why are we doing this? Is it because we have the best interests of the children at heart? What does the Lord expect and want us to do in this situation?*

A debate arose in the year 2000 when a case involving two families in Washington state reached the U.S. Supreme Court. It drew national attention for its emotional consequences. The grandparents sought more visits with their granddaughters after the suicide of their son, the children's father. One of the problems related to the fact that their son and the children's mother were never married. Since the death of their son, the mother of the children married. The grandparents were satisfied with a court-approved arrangement of 26 hours a month, one week in the summer, and special visits on the birthdays of the grandparents. But the mother and her new husband appealed the decision, saying it was excessive and disrupted their family life. The Supreme Court then ruled against the grandparents. In siding with the mother, the court declared that in ordinary circumstances no state law can interfere with the "fundamental right" of parents to make child-rearing decisions. At the same time, the court made clear that in extraordinary circumstances courts may still intervene when grandparents seek visitation rights. Justice Sandra Day O'Connor, in the majority opinion, made it clear that it was not their intent to invalidate all visitation laws, which exist in some form in all 50 states, allowing grandparents to petition to see their grandchildren.

You can see the emotional entanglement. AARP filed an amicus brief supporting the grandparents and praising the court for leaving the door open to less broad visitation laws. "The case was never about taking away parental control," said Cheryl

Matheis, AARP director of state legislation. "It was about giving grandparents a voice in court if there are family troubles and they have exhausted all other ways to stay in touch with their grandchildren."[5]

One family law expert at Duke University weighed in and said, "I love grandparents. They should be involved with their grandchildren's lives. But if the parents object, someone has to decide what's best for the children. And much of society has decided it should be the parents."[6]

Since the high court ruling, some state courts have cited that opinion in deciding challenges to visitation orders, and some experts see the ruling as a setback for grandparent visiting rights, though not necessarily a huge one. Jeff Atkinson, a DePaul University law professor, says that grandparents might have to show an exceptionally close relationship with their grandchildren. The article in the AARP *Bulletin* (as cited in notes 4 and 5) speaks of similar cases and points to laws in all 50 states, with no two states being alike. Meanwhile, the emotional wounds of the legal battles remain open for some; for others, the wounds are beginning to heal.

There are grandparents' movements and support groups throughout the country. If you want to find one, search the Internet. More and more grandparents, angry at being cut off from their grandchildren, whatever the family circumstances, are fighting back and petitioning the courts for visitation rights. With so many homes now fractured by divorce, and with estranged husbands or wives keeping their children away from grandparents as a way of punishing the spouse, some children may never get to know their grandparents—another tragedy from the pandemic divorce rate in this country.

Children born out of wedlock who are abandoned by one parent may never get to know both sets of grandparents. The trend toward unmarried women having children—a fashionable thing to do in today's society—has resulted in hundreds of thousands of children growing up without benefit of the grandparent relationship.

HUMAN HELP IS NOT ENOUGH

Evelyn Christenson speaks about human efforts such as this chapter has described as being, in the final analysis, not enough. This is not to say there isn't a time and place for such efforts by grandparents. But as she points out, "Secular intellectual human help is not sufficient by itself. Only God has the power to reach down and complete the final healing step that mends the broken family members." Why is this true? "Because from the everyday hassles to those devastating family catastrophes, prayer enlists the help of the omnipotent, omnipresent God of the universe who is willing and eager to release His divine power into the lives of our family members. Only God, not humans, can do that!"[7]

As I was writing this, a letter came from a couple in California relating the heartbreak of the death of their daughter leaving behind two children. A week after their daughter's memorial service, they were informed that visitation rights with the children would be allowed only with the children's father present. The scenario was not totally unexpected—their daughter had married a man from a cult. "Our daughter fought for her life for five-and-a-half years [before succumbing to cancer], during which time we helped care for her and the children. After she passed away, we tried to maintain normal contact with our grandchildren, but it became increasingly more difficult, so we decided to follow Matthew 18:15-17." All efforts at reconciliation failed, although these grandparents were persistent and did all the right things. There were attorney and psychologists' fees, court costs, and mandated expenses by the court. In the end, they had to give up the fight. "We have moved on because we have our lives to live.... Our grandchildren live only 15 minutes away, but we haven't seen them in a long time. What we can do and will continue to do is to pray for each of our grandchildren. We have turned them over to the Lord."

"THE NEW FAMILY"?

As more couples divorce and remarry, they create "blended" families of relative strangers, and the odds rise for abuse and betrayal, for strange liaisons and affairs. Dr. Joyce Brothers wrote about this in an article entitled "Terrible Family Secrets." On the surface, some of these new families resemble the traditional nuclear family, with titles of Dad and Mom, Sis and Brother, Uncle and Aunt, Grandma and Grandpa. Dr. Brothers told about an acquaintance, a sociologist, who praised the blended family in a college lecture series she called "The New Family."

"The new family," the sociologist had said, "is blended of people who choose to live together in a manner that is inclusive rather than exclusive. This, the family of the future, is comprised of people who have freely chosen each other. It is held together by choice and caring. Marriage is no requirement."

Dr. Brothers told what happened to this woman, who was married to a college professor, whom she adored, and who had a son, 14. When her husband divorced her and married another woman, who had a 15-year-old daughter, they discovered one of the pitfalls of a blended family. The teenage son began spending most of his time with his new stepsister. When his father and the stepmother separated, the young girl, when she reached 18, married her former stepfather, 43. The son's friends made fun of him. He told his mother, "They say that, since Dad married my sister [stepsister], I'm Dad's brother-in-law—and my own uncle."

Dr. Brothers said her acquaintance might better have entitled her speech "What Can Go Wrong with the New Family." Sometimes where relationships become so ensnarled, incest is a byproduct, Dr. Brothers explained. "The reasoning seems to be: 'Why not? No one's related by blood after all.' But whether related by blood or by familial roles that are legal or assumed, the child is *dependent* upon the adult in psychological, emotional and economic ways." The damage to children is severe and lasting when the boundaries of family roles get blurred within households, whether they are traditional or blended, explains Brothers.[8]

And, one asks, what happens to grandparents in such situations? Dr. Arthur Kornhaber, psychiatrist and president of the Foundation for Grandparenting, says that many times grandparents have been legislated out of existence because of these kinds of problems and situations. "It is always in the best interest of the child to visit with grandparents. It's a deep spiritual bond," he says.

> We live in confusing times; the world's numerous problems can be intimidating. As a grandparent, you face a particularly dizzying array of family situations and social issues—perhaps more than those faced by people in any other group.... Whether you like it or not, nature has placed you in the role of the emotional and spiritual leader of your family. You are the teacher of your children, your grandchildren, and yes, even other people's children and grandchildren.... You represent the past, you are the present and you will determine the future.

These are difficult situations, but being an effective grandparent still means offering unconditional love and being a good role model. Remember, my nurse friend said that, almost without exception, patients and inmates say that the only positive role models in their lives are grandparents. The shape of many of today's families is changing. How can the knowledge of the family's history be transmitted? In situations like these, how do grandparents offer their grandchildren the stability of familial faith?

PUTTING OUR FAITH TO WORK

Living consistently day in and day out and keeping ourselves God-focused offers grandparents incredible opportunities to put our faith to work. Then when we are confronted with the need to be a counselor or we come up against difficult situations, we can offer what our loved ones need.

I asked questionnaire respondents to rate themselves as a faith shaper on a scale of from 1 to 10, with 10 being the highest. Such modesty! Only two grandparents rated themselves a 10. Most felt they were about an 8. Knowing some of these grandparents as I do, and reading between the lines on others, I would easily have ranked them as 10s.

The daughter of missionary parents rated herself a 4 as a faith shaper. Her daughter, at the time she responded, was only 18 months old, but her reasoning went like this: "I believe that a lot is 'caught,' not 'taught,' and until my life spiritually is a 10, I cannot produce a 10. My mother is teaching me about prayer, and I hope that is what I pass on to my daughter as well." (Knowing this young mother and her exceptional grandmother, I can tell you that she would rank as a 10.)

One grandmother summed it up pretty well, reflecting the way so many others felt, when she said, "As a 'faith shaper,' I don't know how I would rate, but I do know that I'm a better grandmother than I was a mother." So many grandmothers told me that!

She continued:

I have learned to be more affectionate, more patient, more willing to play, more free with my time, and more tolerant of apparent wrongdoings. My husband and I do try hard to plant the love of Christ in their lives by means of our own example of living, and in our talking to them. We do not interfere in each family's lifestyle, but we do give suggestions when asked. We do not "preach" to our children or grandchildren, but we accept them as they are. We pray for them diligently, by name, every day.

10

FOREVER, WITH DELIGHT

Blessed is the man who fears the LORD,
Who delights greatly in His commandments.
His descendants will be mighty on earth;
The generation of the upright will be blessed.
—PSALM 112:1-2 (NKJV)

"I remember, and shall forever, with delight, our having Sunday after-church dinner with Grandpa and the Grandmas. That was the most effective way of 'being family' and belonging that I remember from my childhood. Nothing else except Christmas comes close." So wrote my daughter as she reminisced about her beloved Grandpa Pete, Grandma Esther, and Grandma Hattie.

Just thinking about those Sunday dinners now makes me feel surrounded by love. No one could fix

141

roast beef, mashed potatoes, peas and carrots, and salad like Grandma Esther. And always there was vanilla ice cream for dessert with Hershey syrup. Mmm …

Gram never complained; she was always faithful with her Sunday dinners. That was a powerful example of serving others for me. We'd always say how good it was, and she'd always say, "The roast was a little dry," or "The carrots weren't cooked enough," or "The gravy wasn't thick enough." And we'd insist she was wrong, that it was just great! Sweet humility—that was Grandma Esther. It showed how much she wanted to give us her best, but even her best she felt wasn't good enough for us. She loved us so much. It all contributed to that sense that we belonged and that we were children of value to them and to God.

My daughter Rhonda's memories of her Grandma Esther's demonstrations of love brought back a flood of memories to me. Did Grandma know she was providing something so special and memorable for her grandchildren?

CHILDREN OF VALUE

Grandma Esther is no longer living. I can't ask her. But in my heart I feel she did know. She did what she did because of her deep well of love, of course, but also because she recognized the importance of providing a sense of belonging for her grandchildren. She knew it was important to them in the now of their lives and for their future to know and always remember that they were children of value.

Children of value not just to her but to their heavenly Father as well. She was making memories for them—and how they treasure them today!—but she was also building into their subconscious the importance of staying with what their family believes, values, and practices. Grandma Esther was demonstrating familial faith.

My daughter's letter continued:

> You know, Grandma would never sit down herself until everyone had a full plate and was eating.
>
> Grandpa would always pray. Solemn. Or he would ask us to all join hands and say the Lord's Prayer together.
>
> After dinner, Gram would quick get the Bible before everyone was done. She would watch, I think, and when everyone was having their last bite or two, she'd reach for the Bible before anyone got up. Then she'd read or ask someone to read—sometimes it would be one of us kids. But she picked exactly what she wanted everyone to hear that day. It was her time to minister to us all. She never revealed that she was being subtle; otherwise, some of us (as we got older, especially) might have tuned out or rejected it. She never really expounded on what was read, either, but she trusted God with it.

Yes, she did choose exactly what was needed for her family at that particular time. Bearing in mind what had transpired during the week for individual family members, she prayerfully sought God's guidance as to what would minister to certain people, those whom she felt or knew were in greatest need. It may have been a disappointment one of the children had experienced at school or in a sports competition. Perhaps it was a run-in with a teacher or a classmate that the child had shared with her. On the other hand, it may have been something good or exciting that had happened, and Grandma wanted us to recognize God's hand in our lives and His blessing.

In that Sunday after-church group were my own widowed mother and Grandma Esther's unmarried sister, Mildred ("Aunt Mimi," as the children called her). Mimi's life was not easy, working as she did as live-in housekeeper for businesspeople and participating in raising their two children. Grandma Esther wanted to make sure her grandchildren brought joy into Mimi's life, and it was obvious that this was taking place.

Many times there would be others whom Grandpa and Grandma had singled out to be guests—needy people, hurting people. And always there was Aunt Mary, a single woman, a schoolteacher dedicated to her professional calling. Aunt Mary was a delight, endearing herself to her nieces and nephews, always so full of ideas and information, seizing her times with the children as teachable moments. And the kids adored her.

A RICH HERITAGE

"We were family," my daughter underscored the word in her letter.

Sometimes Grandma would send us out to the patio for dessert and coffee while she cleared the table. If we hadn't read the Bible at the table, she'd put it in my hands and show me where to read, or she'd give it to Tonia or Barry.

We all belonged. And it felt so good. Safe. I miss that, Mom. Gives me a lump as I think about it. There was more to Gram than we knew about or recognized at the time. As Grandpa Pete said at her memorial service, "She was a classy lady."

Rhonda has memories of her beloved Grandpa Pete also.

Grandpa was a storyteller. He could tell a yarn and have you laughing, crying, and enthralled for hours. But he was a man's man. A good man. Honest and upright. Knew right from wrong and would speak up about it when the occasion demanded. He was, at the same time, strong, kind, and gentle. He was the best. You know what I got from him? A sense of pride in who I am, my heritage, Christian beliefs, a deep sense of belonging because of it.

When I feel insecure and weak, I think of you, Mom, and Grandpa Pete, Grandma Esther, and Grandma Hattie. Strong people. I can reach back in my memories and say to myself, *My Grandma Hattie was made of strong, good stuff, and so was my Grandpa Pete, and they worked so hard.* I can think to myself: *Look at my grandparents and my children's grandparents and at the heritage they have given to their grandchildren. Someday our children can pass on that heritage to their children, who will be my grandchildren.*

THE DIFFICULT TIMES

Rhonda remembers hearing about the difficult times, how hard it had been at times for her Grandma Hattie, who was widowed in her midthirties and never remarried. "I've got Grandpa Pete's, Grandma Esther's, Grandma Hattie's, your father's, and your blood in my veins, Mom," my daughter says. "I belong to all of you; you belong to me. That's a rich heritage."

And I, her mother, feel undeserving of her accolades. Yet I know that what she says about her grandparents is true, and I am a product of her godly maternal grandmother and the grandfather she never knew. Familial faith has been passed on from one generation to another, and while parental religious heritage is no substitute for a personal relationship with God, these children have made this relationship with their heavenly Father their own through faith in Christ. He is real to them just as He was real to their grandparents and parents. But they saw it lived out in the lives of their grandparents.

The Old Testament prophet Isaiah said a father is to make known the truth to his children (Isaiah 38:19). When this is done, and when these children and grandchildren respond, then the heavenly Father rewards and blesses. We have seen it happen in our family. And reading the letters from those who responded to the questionnaire, I saw how this had happened, and was happening, in those families who understood and followed the biblical mandate.

Powdered Milk and Backyard Gophers

The memories children carry with them of their grandparents are surprising—and often amusing, too. I am sure they would bring smiles to the faces of their grandparents. My mother, for instance, would have thrown back her head and laughed at some of Rhonda's comments.

When I think of Grandma Hattie, I think of powdered milk. Yuck! But you know, she didn't drink much milk and couldn't afford to see it spoil, so being the sensible woman she was, and knowing she needed to have milk for her grandchildren, she kept powdered milk on hand. Grandma was a thinker.

She was also very independent, but maybe because she was a widow, she had to be that way. To me, a child, it seemed how you should be—strong and independent. She was a bit gruff at times and not too mushy, but she was colorful. Such strength of character and love flowed from her. Good and God-fearing, Christ-centered, involved in church activities.

And oh yes, Grandma Hattie loved to watch the roller derby on TV. I can't figure her out on that! Maybe she was a fighter. For sure, she was a survivor.

"Cleanliness is next to godliness." She wrote that, no doubt! (Well, not really, but it sure fit her!)

I remember her fabric scrap boxes in the guest bedroom in her house. She had boxes and boxes of scraps, rolled and rubber-banded, and pinned on each was a piece of paper stating how much was in the little rolled-up batch. So organized!

Maybe that's where my granddaughter Leah gets her sense of orderliness and organization skills. I look at this granddaughter and see traits of my mother, Leah's great-grandmother, and find it just amazing!

Hearing Rhonda talk about her grandmother's fabric scrap boxes brings back a flood of memories. The moment we would land at Grandma Hattie's house, Rhonda would race for the back bedroom and pull out these scrap boxes.

I loved to look through it all—just to see the colors and patterns of the fabric. She'd let me look as long as I'd put it all back just the way I found it. So there I'd be with the stacks—first choice, second choice, and then the yucky pile!

As long as I can remember, this daughter has been interested in interior design. Fabrics are her special delight. Her home is a reflection of her love and appreciation of color and well-coordinated fabrics. Her grandmother would have taken delight in this granddaughter's creativity. But Grandma Hattie was a professional seamstress and for years had acquired and saved the fabric scraps. I remember Rhonda questioning her grandmother one day: "Grandma, did you go to working school?"

My mother repeated the question, pondering how to reply. "Did Grandma go to working school?" And then she told the grandchildren about her growing-up years with a stern father, who was called "Tightwad Teunis" for good reason:

> I wanted to become a nurse, but my mother and father, who were your great-grandparents, thought I should learn how to sew, and so they sent me away to become a seamstress. But you know, God was in on that; He knew what would work out best for me. After my husband died of cancer, and I was left with a baby on the way who was to become your mother, and I had two other children to support, and the Great Depression wiped out everything your grandpa had invested and set aside for us, I had to find a way to make a living. And so I put my sewing skills to work. I made clothes for people—even suits for men. Did I go to working school? Well, I sure worked hard to provide for us. But I liked to sew.

Rhonda remembers something else:

> Oh, the gophers! I was so impressed! My grandma could get gophers. She'd drown 'em! She was so— [struggling for the right word] Grandma was so

multifaceted. Was there anything she couldn't do? She told me once she used to go out on stormy winter nights in Iowa with the town doctor to help deliver babies out in the country. So, you see, she was a nurse, too!

There was no doubt in my mind when she died who she'd lived her life for. I remember coming home from school, learning that Grandma was gone, running up to my room, throwing myself down on my bed, and just sobbing. "Grandma! Grandma!" Then I remember crying out to God, "God, I will always be Your child so I can be with my Grandma again someday." And I meant it. Her influence was that strong on me. I knew I belonged in eternity, in heaven where she was. Since then, I've had my struggles, but I've always thought of Grandma and what she went through and the comfort she had in the Lord—she used to tell us how much God strengthened and helped her. I've thought hundreds of times, *If Grandma Hattie could make it, then so can I. Her blood runs in me!*

I saw tomorrow look at me
from little children's eyes;
and thought how carefully we'd teach
if we were really wise.

—AUTHOR UNKNOWN

In concluding these thoughts on her grandparents and the legacy of their faith, my daughter wrote:

Prayer and reading God's Word and incorporating it into my own life—each grandparent lived those principles for me to see. I observed the result of that commitment and that it was true and good.

And now my children are seeing it in your life, Mom. And they saw it in Dad's and in Grandpa Herman's lives. My prayer is that they will always cherish their memories as much as I cherish mine. Yes, I shall forever, with delight, carry these memories in my heart.

Grandma Hattie's favorite psalm:
The LORD is my light and my salvation;
Whom shall I fear?
The LORD is the strength of my life;
Of whom shall I be afraid? ...
Wait on the LORD;
Be of good courage,
And He shall strengthen your heart;
Wait, I say, on the LORD! (PSALM 27:1, 14, NKJV)

11

THE CROWNS OF GRANDPARENTS

Children's children are a crown to the aged,
and parents are the pride of their children.
—PROVERBS 17:6a

Figure it out: Everybody comes from two parents, four grand-parents, eight great-grandparents, 16 great-great-grandparents, and so on. Every generation back we go, we have twice as many lineal ancestors. Have you ever wondered who, living in Jesus' day, was your lineal ancestor? Was Grandmother Lois in your lineage?

Interesting to think about. The important thing, however, is to make sure that we, as grandparents, reflect the godly qualities that differentiate us from the world in *today's* godless society. Are there biblical precedents of grandparents besides Lois? How about a little quiz?

Who were the grandmothers of these individuals?
- Seth
- Joseph
- Ephraim and Manasseh
- Rehoboam

(Seth had no grandparents. He was the son of Adam and Eve. Joseph's was Rebecca. Ephraim and Manasseh's grandmother was Rachel. Rehoboam's grandmother was Bathsheba.)

Who were these men's grandfathers?
- Benjamin
- Noah
- Isaac
- Esau
- Absalom

(Isaac, Methuselah, Terah, Abraham, and Jesse, respectively.)

All of these people had the Proverbs "crown." Our grandchildren, Proverbs tells us, are "our crowning glory."

Fast-forward into the generations of your immediate forebears. Do you know their stories?

One of my biggest regrets is that I didn't learn more from my maternal grandfather about his life in the Netherlands, his trip over by boat, and his journey inland to the Iowa prairies. My maternal grandmother died when I was in the fourth grade, long before I gave any thought to my ancestry. But I wish that I had questioned my mother more about her parents living in a sod house on the prairie and some of her childhood and later experiences. How difficult was it for my grandfather and grandmother to hang on to their faith when nature seemed to conspire against them, making the dailiness of living so difficult? Did they pore over their Dutch Bible by flickering candlelight to gain hope and strength to go on when the going was so tough? Did their faith flicker like the candle's flame at times?

When I was in high school, we had to write about our ancestors. Grandpa had told me that he came over from the Netherlands on a sailing vessel called the *Potseam* with his father, brothers, and sisters. His mother had died, and they buried her and migrated to the United States. Beyond that, he hadn't told me anything else, and I was too young and unwise to ask for more information. This was unfortunate, because when I was a teenager, Grandpa lived in another town, we didn't have a telephone or a car to visit him, and I realized then that I should have plied him with questions. I turned to my mother, but she wasn't much more informed than I. So I used my imagination and wrote about peripheral things—rosy-cheeked boys and girls skating on the canals in Holland, windmills, and not much of substance. I got an A, and the teacher read the story to all the high school literature classes. I was embarrassed, but at the same time I felt pretty good. It was this same teacher who told me that I needed to cultivate my writing skills and become a writer.

A few years ago my son took me to the Netherlands, and we retraced family roots. It was a wonderful experience. We found the village where this grandpa was born and lived, including the stately old church where the family had worshiped. A caretaker was mowing the churchyard. I mentioned the name Brunsting (I never did learn to speak Dutch). He motioned that we needed to go across the road to the cemetery. As I made my way,

I visualized in my mind's eye my grandfather walking the same way, a young man in the company of other family members going to bury his mother. It seemed to me that almost every plot had the family name. We succeeded in locating my great-grandmother's grave, and it was a touching moment. We were crowning glories for that godly woman buried there.

THE CONNECTEDNESS BRIDGE

A number of questionnaire respondents told me they are researching their predecessors and tracing ancestral lineage. This is a wonderful thing to do, and it is made so much easier today with access through the Internet and other sources.[1] If you don't have a computer, most universities and public libraries make Internet access available for public use. My sister-in-law and I spent some fruitful hours at a library in Iowa, where we attended an Elderhostel event. We tracked down an incredible amount of material, and it was a lot of fun. Of special interest to us was the emphasis on the spiritual life of these ancestors from so long ago as described in newspaper obituaries and in books family members had self-published and given as gifts to the archives of that library. At one point I said to myself, *Wow! Talk about faith!*

It's been said that the life of every man is a diary in which he means to write one story but writes another, and that his saddest hour is when he compares the volume as it is with what he had vowed to make it. Reading about these deceased people made me aware again that the story of our lives is being recorded in God's Book of Life and that that's where it really counts. But it was certainly interesting to read about the activities and interests of my ancestors and their friends and neighbors. These people carried their religious faith with them from the "old country." They left behind a godly heritage.

Many great books and materials (too many to mention) are available to help you in your genealogical research, and they can be purchased at bookstores, at craft centers, or through Internet sources. The suggestions and recommendations such books provide will be helpful to you in correctly preserving cherished things. It is now possible to use archivally safe materials to preserve your family's photos, records, and heirlooms. Enlist the help of your children and grandchildren and create your ancestral history.

Connect with cousins and more distant family members. You might be surprised at how far someone in your family has progressed in tracing the family tree. Family reunions are a great place to make connections. Inheriting old family pictures is helpful, especially when names and dates are written on the back or someone has acquired this information and catalogued it for posterity. Marriage licenses, birth certificates, and documents of this nature can be found in courthouses, if you want to add such items to your family's heritage album. It's disappointing when you can't identify places, dates, and names, if your ancestors are no longer living, so the better part of wisdom is to make sure *now* that your photos are identified. You can make copies of old photos at copy centers and drop them in each child's and grandchild's box (or in their albums, if you are already doing that). Weave genealogy, family lore, and traditions into what you are compiling, and personalize the material as much as possible.

Place a strong emphasis on how faith has carried the family through difficult times.

When my children got married, I gave them the baby books, scrapbooks, and photo albums I had kept for them through the years. In more recent years, I have sorted family photos and mementos acquired since then into boxes labeled for each child and grandchild. Many respondents told me they were doing this. If *you* haven't, consider going through such items and writing appropriate and memorable stories to go along with them. Then give them as gifts at Christmas, birthdays, anniversaries, etc.— they will make a big hit with your family!

If you are a younger mother or grandmother, I encourage you to begin. Since this can be time-consuming, at least label pictures and saved items so that when the day does come that you can devote to this, you will have preserved the necessary information. You might even want to acquire an old trunk at an antique store or yard sale to store these treasures. If not an antique trunk (which can be costly), use sturdy boxes that you can label. But by all means, preserve the connectedness bridge. Some people preserve photo negatives in a fireproof box.

I have found that thinking about the past and recording remembrances is therapeutic for me, and I know it will someday be especially appreciated by my family. The events of our lives and of the lives of those who preceded us make for a sort of blueprint that can endure. I am grateful that I know my ancestors loved the Lord and that I can anticipate meeting them one day in heaven.

The connectedness bridge—the link to family history—is

ours to provide, but we do have to put forth the effort. The importance of the family, its roots and ties even to other countries, is kept in remembrance for future generations when we are diligent to assume the responsibility for preserving this. It does require conscientious effort and can seem a somewhat daunting and overwhelming task. Some selectivity is called for. Ask yourself questions like this: *What will actually have meaning long-term?* The child or grandchild will value his or her childish scrawl and first attempts at writing. I have a file labeled with each grandchild's name into which I drop their letters to me, copies of mine to them, and now copies of the e-mails we've traded. The sentimental Valentines, birthday cards, and special occasion cards have also been sorted and tied with ribbons that will be found in my father's family trunk to be disbursed to family members someday. This kind of thing can be especially meaningful because it tells a story and transmits the love we feel for each other.

Whatever you do, be sure you pass on your reminiscences, the "pages" from your life book that will be meaningful to your grandchildren. If you can't find much from your predecessors, and if you no longer have grandparents or other relatives with whom you can visit, at least make sure that your own life story becomes known to your loved ones. What do you include? The most important aspect of the heritage you pass on to your grandchildren relates to what God has done in your life, what you have learned, and what you hold dear. What are your favorite verses, passages, stories in the Bible? What are some of your favorite songs—old hymns, praise songs, anthems? When did you invite Christ into your heart?

In their book *Your Heritage,* Otis Ledbetter and Kurt Bruner talk about the intentional impression points we make in the lives of others, that is, how we impress upon others our values, preferences, and concerns. And we do it through our talk and our actions. It's done intentionally and incidentally. We see this in the life of Moses and the commands God gave through him to the Jewish people who had escaped Pharaoh's rule: "Love the LORD your God with all your heart and with all your soul and with all your strength. These commandments that I give you today are to be upon your hearts. *Impress them on your children"* (Deuteronomy 6:5-7, emphasis added).

A spiritual legacy is the process whereby parents [and grandparents] model and reinforce the unseen realities of the spiritual life.

—J. OTIS LEDBETTER AND KURT BRUNER, *YOUR HERITAGE: HOW TO BE INTENTIONAL ABOUT THE LEGACY YOU LEAVE*

THE MISSING LINK

I read a delightful account in *The Dallas Morning News* that points up how good it is to share your life stories with grandchildren—and also to share some far-fetched, fun stories with them. A grandfather wrote of the Sunday morning journey his mother took him on when, in his 10th year, they went to pay homage to the family patriarch:

By taking me to visit Grandpa Conner, who was born in 1870, [my mother] gave me a gift more important than a winning lottery ticket or a trip to Disney World. She gave me the gift of a sense of my place in the family and community. Now, for my children and grandchildren, I am a direct link to that world of the 19th century.

There is a widespread feeling of dismay today of spiritual disconnection, an emptiness that is only partially filled by the national common experience of watching the Super Bowl and the Academy Awards on television. These rituals and others like them place us in time and tie us to our contemporaries on a superficial level but soon become old news and are forgotten. They are rituals in search of a myth, and a myth-less society is in danger of becoming neurotic, insane, even suicidal.

He told of his grandpa sitting on the front porch, in an out-sized rocker, wearing the uniform of the 19th-century farmer—overalls, long-sleeve cotton shirt buttoned at the wrists and collar, and clodhopper boots. "At his side lay Judy, a small terrier." And then one day his grandpa told him a wild tale of "Judy and her man-killing ways." It was a crazy made-up story that had the 10-year-old lad all ears.

He said his mother was seldom conscientious of her other parental duties and had never read a book on any subject. And then he made this observation:

By taking a fatherless boy on these Sunday pilgrimages, was she but re-enacting the journeys she had taken as a young girl to the home of her own great-grandparents? How could she have known but through wisdom borne by family, the importance of these journeys into the life of a man of the 19th century, to hear his myths, and someday pass them on to succeeding generations?

For who could ever be very impressed with the mundane doings of Seinfeld's family or Roseanne's or the intimate strangers of *Survivor* when they have been to the 19th century and shared the same porch with man-killing Judy (no bigger than a loaf of bread) and lived to tell it?[2]

"WHEN MY CHILDREN WERE AROUND ME"

And then there's the story of a biblical grandpa. He's sitting on the ash heap, an older man reminiscing, the patriarch of patience, but not without some longing and mourning—a nostalgic recital, a look back at the panorama of his life. He's Job, of course, discoursing about the days of his prime, and it's pretty sad. Let's listen in:

How I long for the months gone by,
for the days when God watched over me,
when his lamp shone upon my head
and by his light I walked through darkness!

Oh, for the days when I was in my prime,
when God's intimate friendship blessed my house,
when the Almighty was still with me
and my children were around me. (Job 29:1-5)

The story of his losses and the disruption in his family life is well known. He lived in the lap of luxury. He had it all (read the opening chapters of the book of Job). But in one fell swoop, it was all taken away. This godly man, called by God "blameless and upright, a man who fears God and shuns evil" (Job 1:8), was stripped of all his possessions, including his sons and daughters, who were killed in a Texas-style tornado. God allowed Satan to do it with one proviso: "He is in your hands; but you must spare his life" (2:6). One wonders, did he lose grandchildren, too?

His wife survived and goaded him, "Are you still holding on to your integrity? Curse God and die!" (2:9).

How did Job handle that? He responded to his wife, "You are talking like a foolish woman. Shall we accept good from God, and not trouble?" And we are told that "in all this, Job did not sin in what he said" (2:10).

After allowing Satan to do this to His servant Job, the Lord blessed the latter part of Job's life more than the first. At the end of the story we learn that Job lived to be 140 and saw his children and their children to the fourth generation (Job 42:12,16). Imagine it—he had great-great-great-great-grandchildren!

The point in bringing up the story of this venerated patriarch is to recognize, as Job mentioned, that when the children are about you, you have an unequaled opportunity to leave an impression upon their lives. Your grandchildren are going to learn; the hearts and minds of these impressionable children are going to be filled with something. They are going to learn from others. The question is not, will they learn? The right question is, what will they learn and from whom? Your grandchildren's hearts are going to be inclined. Which way? How? As a grandparent, you can serve many purposes, creating many impression points. You don't have to be authoritarian; you can offer understanding, comfort, love, experiences, hugs, and a sense of strength and stability for each family member.

Training a child in "the way he should go" means, among other things, taking into account the bent—the inclinations, habits, and interests—of the child, in keeping with his mental and physical development. Childhood is the time for training. But you are not the parent; you are the grandparent. You can enhance a grandchild's life, but you cannot direct it. Interference by grandparents can cause family problems—wounded feelings, resentments, hurt feelings. We need to be cautious about interfering.

A friend groaned over the phone one day, sharing her heartache about a young adult grandchild, and then asked, "How far can I go? What can I do? What must I say?"

Our children and grandchildren may interpret what we do and say as intrusion. They do not always appreciate "advice meant for your own good." Caution! Is direct intervention ever warranted? If we see that our family members are harming themselves, being abusive, or being abused, then yes, appropriate intervention is warranted.

How Far Can a Grandparent Go?

Frequently, in my research, I read or heard almost the same thing: "How far can a grandparent go?" As grandparents, we cannot always train, and we shouldn't be preachy, but we can certainly instill Christian values by our example. Parents are told to train their children in the way they *should* go, not the way they may *want* to go. While the children are about us, they need guidance in the right way. Be discerning about the difference between intrusion and involvement. If you are baby-sitting and the need presents itself for discipline, reinforce what you know the parents would do or say. Don't undermine their directives, but be firm and take control. Relinquish control when the parents are there. Seek to make your role one of approval, of loving delight in the child, and of reliable support and respect for the parents. If you can do this, you will become important and dearly loved by your children and grandchildren.

One grandmother was told by her son-in-law that she wasn't to discuss things "religious" with his children (her grandchildren), and her daughter informed her that for sake of peace in the home, her mother needed to comply. The grandmother accepted this. But like many other grandparents, she gave the grandchildren Christian books, videos, and games at gift-giving times. These gifts were received by the children with joy and were accepted by her daughter and son-in-law without fuss. "But when my grandchildren reached 18," she said, "they were young adults. I took each of them out for lunch after their birthdays and said, 'There's something that's been missing in your life and your education. Now that you are of age, I am going to tell you what the Lord means to me.'" And she said it was "absolutely wonderful!" The grandchildren said, "Oh, Grandma, we know how much you love Jesus!" But now she knew that they understood and she had the joy of leading each one to pray to receive Christ. "I want my grandchildren in heaven with me someday," she said quietly.

Another friend wrote that one of her granddaughters, a college graduate working in the "big city," isn't attending church. My friend recalled, "I sent her a letter that said: 'I wonder if you are taking time these days for a quiet time? Beginning each day with your Bible and prayer is such a lift. I'm enclosing a copy of the little booklet [*Our Daily Bread*] Grandpa and I read together each morning. It's an introductory issue. You can send in for it if you'd like to get it each month.'"

Notice that they didn't subscribe to it for her. They weren't going to force something on her that she might not read and that she might resent. This granddaughter has been raised in a home where she had the example of parents who read the Bible, devotional books, and good Christian literature. Her parents, grandparents, and great-grandparents had handed her a heritage of faith. Her living progenitors were praying for her. She knew it. She now had the freedom to choose. She had a strong foundation for understanding and responding to the work of God in her life. She had been trained right.

Never underestimate the importance of the training that you gave your children and that, hopefully, they passed on to their children, your grandchildren. The home and environment in which children are trained make deep and lasting impressions. It is the Word of God that is the basic element of godly living. When given to our grandchildren by words and through our actions and lifestyles, that is, by our example, such training can take hold. But what if it doesn't? Parents are responsible to be faithful in their training; they are not responsible for results once that child reaches the age of maturity. Then it is that we use the strong arm of prayer.

I send letters to my grandchildren. They've each been raised in a Christian home, but peer pressure and the influence of the media are so pervasive that I seize every opportunity to communicate with them. To open a letter from Grandma, or maybe a silly card that's just perfect for them, they have to take time for that—and Grandma is "in their face" in a loving, good-natured way. For example, I sent my granddaughter a cute card showing a tiny cat in a flowerpot. Inside, it said, "I grew a cat just for you!" It made a huge hit! I had "inherited" Leah's calico when her brother had cancer and they had to part with their indoor cats.

And always, with my letters, I include a Bible verse and something meaningful that suits the recipient. Verses from the book of Proverbs are so good. And here's something else that works: I keep a 9-by-12-inch envelope at my desk with each child's name on it that I drop newspaper and magazine clippings in when I come across something that fits the grandchild. I put a little sticky note on when the envelope has a few of these goodies, and it will say something like "Just to let you know I've been thinking of you." I've been doing the same thing for my children for years. My daughter will inevitably call to say, "Oh, Mom, you've been thinking of me." You'd better believe it! Are these children and grandchildren really ever out of our head (or hair!) and hearts? Once a parent, always a parent; once a grandparent, always a grandparent! You never stop being either one. The cord is cut, but not the relationship.

Upon giving my new grandmother friend, Beverly Montgomery, a book to read with her new grandson, she wrote a sweet thank-you note to me in which she said, "I had no idea how much I would love our precious Hamilton, or how much of my 'thought life' he would consume. What a joy!" Every time a child is born, a grandparent is born too. And that grandchild is from that moment on always in our thoughts.

Dr. Louis Paul Lehman, pastor of Calvary Church, Grand Rapids, Michigan, provided this illustration many years ago: If you knew that your child at 22 years of age would be thrown into the water and drown, what would you do when the child is five years old? Would you try to keep him away from the water, or would you train him to swim? You might not be able to prevent his being thrown into the water, but you would be able to prevent his drowning if he had been taught how to swim.

You know that your children and grandchildren are going to be thrown into this world with all its hazards. They will become part of life and death. Some things are inescapable. They will meet sorrow and joy. Sin and temptation will lure them. They will know the conflict of duty and pleasure. They will partake of living and, eventually, of dying—"after this the judgment" (Hebrews 9:27, KJV). They can become responsible individuals because right now you, as grandparent, have the privilege of participating in their upbringing.

Some grandparents are so fearful of meddling that they skirt the major issues that need to be addressed. Caring is not meddling. Providing sound advice is not intruding. Live with your conscience. Say and do the right things.

When it comes to leaving our grandchildren an example they can follow to faith in Christ, our desire should be like the one held by many grandparents I talked to who said, in effect, "I want to leave an influence for righteousness."

THE ANCHOR OF FAITH

Dr. T. Berry Brazelton, professor of pediatrics at Harvard Medical School and chief of child development at Boston Children's Hospital during the late 1990s, emphasized the need for grandparents to be as a cushion protecting families battered by breakups, financial woes, unrelenting schedules, and work pressures. "The nuclear family is a lonely one," he said, pointing out that each generation in our culture searches for its own values. But without the last generation as a backup, young families can feel anxious and without an anchor. "Grandparents can convey what their family stands for by letting grandchildren into their lives and past. By passing on your family's history and beliefs, you'll teach your grandchildren that there's more to family life than surviving day to day."

God's purpose for families extends across generations. It's been said that as we age, if we put our stories in the bank (that is, the hearts and minds of loved ones), they can gather interest in deepening meaning. So make sure the connectedness bridge spans the generations as a link to familial history. Above all, make certain the baton of faith is passed on.

All the days ordained for me
were written in your book
before one of them came to be.
—PSALM 139:16

12

A GRANDPARENT'S ESSENCE

And live a life of love, just as Christ loved us and gave himself up for us as a fragrant offering and sacrifice to God.
—EPHESIANS 5:2

Grandparents are influential whether they mean to be or not. Certain smells, for instance, trigger memories. Some of the warmest memories my questionnaire respondents shared with me related to the fragrance of a grandmother—and not just the department store variety of fragrance.

Martha Ashworth wrote:

Memories of my Grandmother Martha bring back a flood of special warm feelings. After all these years of her being with the Lord, I still miss her. When I am asked about my name, I state that, like my grandmother,

I'm a typical "Martha" personality, as described in the Bible. I know I was blessed to be named after such a great lady as Grandma Martha.

Today, Granddaughter Martha is a dynamo doer, petite, vivacious, and fun to be around. But there is a sweetness and a depth to her that caused me to wonder how she attained such qualities.

In the eyes of the world, she probably would have been classified as insignificant, but the impact she made on my life was very significant. She lived her faith in such a way that it's stayed with me through the years.

Grandpa was quiet and often sat reading his Bible, but Grandma was busy and vivacious. Whether she was teaching me how to dust furniture, letting me climb on the stool to reach her old wooden phone mounted on the wall and ring the operator, or reminding me it was time for our afternoon Coke and her big homemade sugar cookies, she was just fun to be around.

I associate certain smells with my grandmother and her loving touch, but they aren't perfume or store-bought fragrances. Instead, I feel a warmth that brings a smile as I recall the smell of freshly plowed dirt from the garden outside my grandparents' dining room window, the mustiness of the fruit cellar, and the subtle odor of gas emitted from the little open burner stove in the bathroom. These may not be the scents one usually associates with a grandmother's love, but for me as an adult, these olfactory imprints bring up the joy I cherish as I remember the essence of my godly grandmother and grandfather.

Who would have thought that their values, their love, their spirituality would be neatly packaged into such simple memories? For example, when I think about one smell, my nose actually detects it in a daily activity, then their entire legacy floods into my mind—all they were and all they represented. I think it's childhood and the small, seemingly insignificant pieces of what's going on about us that form the complete puzzle for us as adults. Memories—they are so important!

Reflections of my godly grandmother bring to mind a joy and nostalgia that few other things in life offer.

—MARTHA ASHWORTH

How right she is. Martha's story was repeated in myriad ways by others who happily shared their memories of grandparents and the essence of their faith and love that imparted a sweet-smelling fragrance, as it were, that lingers in the lives of grandchildren to this day. Grandparents who gave so lovingly of themselves can be likened to what the apostle Paul talked about when he remembered the generosity of those who sent gifts to him through Epaphroditus. "I have received full payment and even more.... They are a fragrant offering, an acceptable sacrifice, pleasing to God" (Philippians 4:18).

My dear friend Phyllis speaks lovingly of her grandmother's hospitality:

> Grandma was hospitable, and her example of hospitality in the home was passed on to me. It seemed no one was ever a stranger. My grandparents' home was always a haven of rest for adults and children, whether that involved taking in members of the family who might need temporary help, feeding family and friends because they needed it, or entertaining others on social occasions.
>
> One of my personal favorites at Grandma's was what she called "a piece." A piece was simply a large slice of homemade bread thickly spread with butter and sprinkled with sugar. How tasty that was, and what a treat for we youngsters! I can still see myself in that large, warm kitchen, sitting at the round oak table and licking my lips, and Grandma enjoying every minute of it.

Otis Ledbetter and Kurt Bruner *(Your Heritage: How to Be Intentional About the Legacy You Leave)* emphasize that family fragrances go deeper than the senses; they have a lot to do with the three legacies—emotional, spiritual, and social—that we leave to our families. It has everything to do with demonstrative love (and grandparents are so good at doing that—the hugs, the kisses, the hand holding, the pats on the back, the touching that is so warm, loving, and important); with the respect we show to one another, honoring each other's worth; with the peace that characterizes a well-ordered home (don't major on the minors!); with a healthy dose of merriment (joy and laughter); and with affirmation and praise (encouragement).

Martha wisely adds that it is with some trepidation that she wonders about the legacy she is leaving in the minds of her grandchildren.

What may seem insignificant from my perspective could be creating lifetime impressions in them. How will they remember me? What senses will bring forth in them the essence of what they recall as "Mema." I pray that somewhere within that total memory will be the values I hold dear and try to pass on to each of them.

I would hope my faith in the face of adversity would be foremost in their minds as a pattern for them to follow in those difficult times that will come into their lives at some point. However, when I recently inquired of my 11-year-old grandson what he thought he would remember about me, he said simply watching movies with me. Perhaps that can be translated into time spent together. Or was it only significant because we'd watched an old movie together the night before? Hopefully, as he reaches adulthood, there will be more than surface activities in the heritage I pass along.

There are many missed opportunities in our parenting and grandparenting, but I believe that one crystallized moment can bring back the total essence of all we are trying to create as we pass on the legacy of our faith to the next generation.

As a grandparent, I see what opportunities I missed with my children. But I think grandchildren are God's way of saying, "I love you so much that I'm giving you another opportunity to take advantage of special moments to make lifetime memories." Hopefully, through our godly grandparenting, our precious grandchildren can catch a glimpse of God.

A faint aroma of gingerbread and all good things mixed together seems to linger all around a grandmother.
—ELIZABETH GORDON, AGE 12

I loved their home. Everything smelled older, worn but safe, the food aroma had baked itself into the furniture.
—SUSAN STRASBERG, FROM "BITTERSWEET"

Some grams smell of lavender soap, some grams smell of French perfume. My gram smells of pastry and new bread and peppermints. My gram smells gorgeous.   —PETER

THE ESSENCE OF GRANDMOTHERLY
AUNT DORA

Aunt Dora, my father's sister, was more like a grandma to me than an aunt probably because I never knew my paternal grandmother, since she died before I was born. My father's sister, her husband, and their children were the relatives who maintained a close relationship with my mother after his death. Getting to visit Aunt Dora and Uncle Bert was a favorite treat for me as a child. They were something else!

Whenever I am near a fragrance counter in a department store, I wander over to the eau de cologne section, where the old-fashioned bottles of imported German cologne can still be found (in some stores.) Anytime I knew we were going to visit Aunt Dora, I begged Mama for one of her hankies. This dear aunt would take me by the hand, lead me to her bedroom, and say, "Now give me your hankie," and she would pour out some of this cologne, which came from "the old country," she explained. If I didn't have a hankie, she always managed to pull one from her dresser drawer. Ah, the essence of that dear grandmotherly aunt!

To this day, I love walking through the cosmetics department in stores and sampling the fragrances. At Christmastime one year, my granddaughter Christa sent me a pretty little satin bag full of fragrance samples. On the gift card she had written, "To my smelly Grandma!" and I laughed, happily remembering our excursions through the stores getting all "smelled up." Memories!

Aunt Dora also had an old pump organ, which she would let me pump and try to play. (She had a disabled daughter, Maggie, and the story of these two awesome women is told in the next chapter by Maggie's daughter.) As I reflect on my relatives, I would have to say that no one made an impression upon my heart and mind as a small child quite like this dear, faith-filled aunt. The whole time I was with Aunt Dora, she would be hugging and loving me and telling me about my daddy and how he loved Jesus. Is it any wonder I wanted our family to go and live with her, Uncle Bert, and those thoughtful cousins?

THE ESSENCE OF GRANDMOTHER RUTH

Another questionnaire respondent, Ruth, was named after her grandmother.

> My Grandmother Ruth was a strong Christian, but in her day, faith in Christ was not something one discussed. She made it very obvious, however, that Christ was her living Savior and the Lord of her life. He had made her a different person than most adults I knew as a child. She asked forgiveness when she felt she might have hurt someone by something she said or did—she was just so conscientious that way. She took whatever came her way with a calm, peaceful spirit. I was with her at a candlelight service on New Year's Eve when I accepted Christ into my life. I haven't been the same since, but she was my role model and heroine. When she died, my grandfather told my mother that he wanted to go where she had gone, and he asked Christ into his life.
>
> Because of my legacy from Grandmother Ruth, I have been careful to let my children and grandchildren know what Christ means to me and what He is doing in our lives. When they come to visit, we sit around

and talk about how we can be used in our spheres of influence to reach others. I am so thankful that all of our daughters have led people to Jesus through their words and actions, and also our granddaughters have led their friends to the Lord and encouraged other friends in that direction. We remind our grandchildren that God has planned good works for them to do and has a plan for their lives.

When one of our granddaughters was 10 days old, she had heart surgery. I spent a lot of time with her and my daughter, taking care of them. When God spared her life, I knew He had great plans for her, and we have reminded her of that, and she understands. It's so important for grandparents to be there for the grow-ing-up years of these precious grandchildren, to take an interest in what's going on in their lives at each stage, and to understand how they think. I have encouraged my daughters to read and learn about the temperaments, spiritual giftedness, and birth order of each of their children and to take these things into consideration as they parent them individually. My husband and I have done that, and it's helped us in our grandparenting.

What wise grandparents this couple are! How blessed their grandchildren are to have grandparents to whom they can look for nurturing and guidance. "We have to be lights for them in a dark world," this Grandmother Ruth wrote to me.

"I Felt Safe at My
Grandparents' Home"

Vicki, who grew up in a home with a mother who suffered from clinical depression, wrote touchingly about her grandmother, another Grandma Ruth.

By the age of eight, I was already seasoned at being the new kid and usually entered into the experience in a fairly assertive manner—introducing myself, initiating interaction. I was born into a military family, and so being new was an ongoing experience and knowing how to make new friends quickly was a form of survival. Yet I have one memory of being new that stands out in my mind with a different flavor from the rest. It is a memory that I had forgotten until fairly recently, yet the recalling of it helps me to see aspects of my Christian journey more clearly.

I see myself in my mind's eye entering timidly into a Sunday school classroom. A picture of Jesus is on the wall. I remember knowing that the man in the picture was Jesus, but I'm not sure how I know. Chairs are lined up and several kids are already seated. My grandmother motions for me to take a seat. I sit down in the second row next to a quiet-looking girl. I am uncharacteristically cautious. I am apprehensive.

My grandmother wears her dark-brown hair short and permed. Her large, intense, brown eyes shine behind glasses that sometimes slip down her nose. She wears housedresses at home, but this day she is wearing a suit and heels. My mother, sister, and brother and I have flown out from Colorado to see her. It is only the second time I remember visiting with her. She and my grandfather, "Dado," live in the San Francisco area in a cute little house with a backyard garden filled with snapdragons, which fascinate me with their opening and closing "mouths."

I feel safe at my grandparents' home. Their home is cheerful and tidy, and my grandmother cooks wonderful Southern meals. There is always a tablecloth on their dining room table. Though in my family I was the middle child and remember feeling a certain hunger for attention, here, with my grandmother, I have a special status because of our history. She had taken care of me during the first year of my life. My father was an air force military officer, called to fight in the Korean War, and my mother had gone to be with her parents for the duration of my father's assignment. During that time, I was born. My mother experienced a difficult delivery and, so I was told, my grandmother took over my care for the first eight months of my life while my mother recovered.

Now I am eight and visiting this special grandmother of mine. My grandmother goes to the front of the Sunday school classroom. She nods to a woman who is playing the piano and everyone starts to sing. I move my mouth, pretending that I know the words, since everyone else seems to know them and I don't want to stand out.

Then my grandmother begins to tell the story of a poor woman who has only one penny and who gives her only penny to Jesus. I stare at the picture on the wall and wonder why the woman wanted to give it to Him. From the tone of my grandmother's voice, I can tell that it is a good thing to do. I remember wondering what Jesus did with the money. Then a basket is passed around, and we are told to put our money into the basket for Jesus. I have a dime that I have been holding tightly. My hands are hot and sweaty from holding the dime so long, and I remember being glad to release it into the basket. Holding it had become a burden.

Then my grandmother tells the class that I am her granddaughter and that my name is Vicki. Everyone looks at me. I want to get up and hide behind my grandmother, my "Nanny." But here, at this church, she is the teacher, and though I am only eight, I realize that she has to treat me like everyone else. Nevertheless, when she introduces me, I can tell that she is proud of me. Her eyes glisten when she says my name, and I am proud of her, too, for being the teacher. I remember feeling that she was teaching something very important. I wouldn't have been able to explain why—it was just a feeling.

That is all I remember. I don't know the details of whether my grandmother told me more about Jesus at her house in preparation for going with her to church. I don't remember if she prayed with me.

Unfortunately, I didn't get another extended stay with my grandmother until I was a teenager. My third visit with her was also positive, and with that visit, again, I remember feeling safe and loved. Though she was no longer a Sunday school teacher, I knew that she was a Christian, and I knew that God made a difference in her life. I do remember that during that visit we prayed together. I did not accept Christ into my life until a few years later, but I have no doubt that my grandmother helped, by her example, to open my eyes to the Lord.

Taking classes at a church with a friend when I was in elementary school also helped me in my growth. And in my teen years, seeing a skit about Jesus in Young Life made me think. In other words, I believe that my grandmother planted the seed, other Christians watered it, and the Holy Spirit convicted me one night as I read the Gospel of John. Then in California, as a young adult, I stepped up in front of a church body and confessed Jesus as Lord and Savior. For me, coming to the Lord was a process. My grandmother was an important part of that process. She was the first person I remember who showed me, by both her actions and teachings, that Jesus was about love and provision.

When Vicki was 21, her mother took her life. This was a sad and difficult time for Vicki. That story is told in chapter 14, in which she was willing to reach back into her memory bank to retrieve thoughts about her grandmother and how she handled the suicide death of her daughter. "My grandmother, Ruth Byrd Ward, was a strong woman," Vicki says. "I like the fact that she'll be honored by being included in your book."

Vicki concludes her letter to me this way: "I think a lot about releasing. That little girl who was so relieved to release the dime into the offering plate is still within me. I want to release my hurts, my fears, my anxieties to Jesus. I also want to be like the poor woman who gave her Lord everything. That is my prayer. *I give You my life, Lord. I trust You to take care of me. Thank You for grandparents. Thank You for Christian community. I love You. Use me, Lord. Use my life to Your glory. Amen.*"

LASTING IMPRESSIONS

Charlotte Moss, a decorator and retailer, writes about the lasting impressions that influence our homes and how we decorate them and about how these influences follow us throughout our lives. She writes lovingly about her grandmother's cottage on the Potomac River and her grandmother's house in the city:

> ...filled with pictures, lace-draped tables, squashy comfortable chairs, and lots of books...The bathrooms were stocked with creams, lotions, and soaps of all shapes, colors, and fragrances. I loved spending the night there because she would let me stay in the bath forever....
>
> I remember the comfortable, welcoming smell of

the kitchen, where there was always something baking in the oven. In the musty attic I would hide for hours reading my mother's childhood scrapbooks and trying on my grandmother's hats and shoes from the twenties and thirties. My grandmother kept everything. I guess her attic was her diary.[1]

Her reflections brought back a flood of memories of the home where I spent the first 11 years of my life, especially the attic and my father's beautiful old trunk. I loved sitting in the attic, the light dangling from the rafters, and looking at all the things stored in the trunk. Today that trunk is one of the most-loved items in my bedroom. Inside, in the lid, my father's signature can be seen. As a child, I would sit with his photo in my hand and gaze longingly at his signature. These are lasting impressions that influence not only our homes and how we decorate them but even our very being.

WARMTH AND SIMPLICITY

Simpler times, gentle graces, hard times, the Depression era, a time when time itself seemed to stand still, crank telephones, coal-oil lamps, woodstoves and base burners with isinglass "windows," summer canning, threshing crews on the farm, family reunions, taffy pulls on cold winter evenings, sledding on the hills, ice skating, sleigh riding, quilting bees—these are some of the memories people recalled when writing about the fragrance and essence of grandparents.

Dennis Rainey wrote about canoeing trips he and his wife,

Barbara, took with their family, including playing King of the Rock, accompanied by much laughter and fun. "Just the smell of the river reminded me of being a kid again."

Grandparents wrote about whitewater trips on the Colorado River with their families, including having water fights, setting up camp, roasting marshmallows—all the fun things done on such outings. When family vacation traditions include Grandma and Grandpa, the nostalgia sweeps over you as you look back in time.

One of the daughters of retired missionary friends wrote:

> Memories of my grandparents come often. Memories of their home are of warmth and simplicity. Material-ism has never been a part of their lives; after all, they lived through the Depression and lost everything, including Grandma's "dream home," which she points out when we drive down that street, but always to say, "The Lord gives, and the Lord takes away."

Did Grandma Piersma ever think that her granddaughter would still be quoting her more than 30 years later?

> She told us stories about the Depression, emphasizing how happy a family could be with little when they had each other. She said they always had something to eat, and then she'd add, "Because the Lord was our provider."

Granddaughter Anne remembered also the Bible being read once a day around the kitchen table, "along with the *Daily*

Bread devotional book." She recalled with pleasure Grandma's storytelling skills:

> She was the best storyteller and Bible reader! She made Bible characters come alive. And oh, the missionary stories! They were so interesting. She always worked with Pioneer Girls and in Vacation Bible School. I remember an object lesson she gave about someone who was caught cheating. I knew I'd never cheat after hearing what Grandma had to say about it!

This grandma loved playing games with her granddaughters. Scores of people remember with pleasure the games—Parcheesi, Old Maid, checkers, dominoes, Chinese checkers, Monopoly.

"A Warmth and Aroma"

As adolescents, Anne and her sister(s) were separated many years from both parents and grandparents when they attended a boarding school for missionary children. "We found out 'by mistake' that Grandpa and Grandma paid our tuition because Mom and Dad couldn't afford it." This was sacrificial giving on the part of these grandparents, but oh, how God blessed in the missionary work of their son and his wife, who served in a hostile environment for many years! And also, how the grandparenting of these grandparents helped their lovely granddaughters become godly young women who married and established Christian homes.

I went to college near where Grandpa and Grandma lived, so once again their home became my refuge on weekends. There was such a warmth and aroma that flowed from that little home. Anyone could shed the stress of daily life and relax as soon as walking through their door.

And there it was again, the emphasis on "the warmth and aroma," the sweet-smelling fragrance of love that so many wrote to me about. These were questionnaire respondents who didn't know each other, who had no idea what someone else was saying, yet I found this emphasis in letter after letter. This essence of godly grandparenting remains long after other memories fade.

Anne explained that in their later years she saw how the relationship between her grandparents got sweeter and sweeter. "It was a lesson to me that marriage can get better and better when the Lord is in control." Her grandfather had to become her grandmother's eyes when she started losing her sight; her grandmother had to become his ears when he lost much of his hearing. "They were so grateful to have each other and gave the Lord the credit."

She spoke of the values that were passed on, including a work ethic. "Grandfather used to say, 'Work never hurt anyone.'"

From her grandparents and parents, Anne acquired habits that she carried with her into her own marriage and the home she and her husband established—habits that include prayer and Bible reading and gathering the family around the dinner table each evening.

I remember how we stayed at the table sometimes until nine in the evening, just reading the Bible and talking about the Lord. We still do that, especially when all the family come from distances to be together for a holiday or some event.

Our social life, growing up, was centered around the church and its activities. Hospitality was always our lifestyle, including taking meals to the sick and adding an extra plate at meals with little or no notice. Acquiring a good education and reading the best books were very important.

Do you see a pattern here? Those who were trained according to the biblical precepts acquire habits that they carry with them into adulthood. That is how we can carry on the flame of faith from generation to generation. Parents and grandparents who do this are doing exactly what Psalm 78 tells them to do.

> *I will utter hidden things, things from of old—*
> *what we have heard and known,*
> *what our fathers have told us.*
> *We will not hide them from their children;*
> *we will tell the next generation*
> *the praiseworthy deeds of the LORD,*
> *his power, and the wonders he has done....*
> *He commanded our forefathers*
> *to teach their children,*
> *so the next generation would know them,*

even the children yet to be born,
and they in turn would tell their children.
Then they would put their trust in God
and would not forget his deeds
but would keep his commands.
(Psalm 78:2b-7)

13

LOVE'S LEGACY

This is the day the LORD has made;
let us rejoice and be glad in it.
—PSALM 118:24

My cousin once removed Theodora DeGraaff Kracht wrote lovingly about her grandmother Dora Westra Van Batavia and her mother, Maggie Van Batavia DeGraaff (my first cousin).

"Only one life, 'twill soon be past; only what's done for Christ will last." My grandma was such a special lady. That motto was on the wall in her home. When Grandma died, my mom got it, and so I grew up with it. Grandma had many favorite Bible verses, but Psalm 118:24 was one she loved, and she would say, "Be happy in the Lord!" She would recite favorite little poems and scriptures to us. "Each season has its tasks; each reaps its own rewards; but let us not forget the

191

giving was the Lord's." That was Grandma. She was always so happy—happy in the Lord and happy with her husband and family. You always left her presence with a little gift. Usually it included a small Christian storybook. She and Grandpa went out of their way to make others happy.

I share those memories and can still see, in my mind's eye, that beautifully scripted motto on the wall of my Aunt Dora's home. I can still hear this dear grandmother reciting her little poems and Bible verses for us. I always listened attentively. This special lady must have been Mrs. God to a father-hungry little girl. I intuitively knew she somehow had a special connection with Mr. God.

Houses are made of brick and stone,
Homes are made of love alone.

Theodora continued:

That little motto [above] was also on the wall at Grandma's house. It described our home life. We were blessed to live in a home filled with love, laughter, and concern for one another and others.

I grew up during World War II, and those were difficult times. The Chicago, Milwaukee, and St. Paul train ran through Hull, Iowa, where we lived, twice daily. Beggars (some called them "bums"; others called them "hoboes") who hitched rides on these trains would stop by our home and ask for a hand-out. Mom and Dad never said no. Mom would say in Dutch, "Eine hanse stucke broet" (One hand slice bread), "Twie hanse stucke broet" (Two hands slice bread). Of course they always answered "Two!" Then she would slice her fresh-baked bread and share with them.

Sometimes she would give them potatoes so they could take them back to their campfires along the rail-road tracks outside of town and bake them in the coals. But we were learning something: It is more blessed to give than to receive. In serving others, we serve the Lord and we are blessed in the loving and giving. We saw the Golden Rule lived and practiced.

Her recollections paint a portrait of the selfless love of godly grandparents as well as the Eunice-like mother and father she had. Her memories reveal the fun-loving people they also were.

At Grandpa and Grandma's house, we always had prayer before and after meals. Grandpa would ask God to bless the food before we ate, and thank Him for it, and then afterward he would read the Bible. And then he would say, "What was the last word?" and we had better have listened because you never knew whose name he was going to call. One time a cousin whis-pered to me, "Say, 'Mosquito,'" which I did loudly and clearly. As a result, Grandpa read the passage over again....When he was all finished, then he would close by praying for other things—the crops, the need for rain, the needs of family members, neighbors, the church, missionaries. No one and nothing was over-looked.

These were Iowa folk—good, hardworking farmers, with the neatest, cleanest farms you would ever hope to see. It's how I grew up, so I easily identified with what she was saying. Going to visit on the farms of aunts and uncles was the highlight of my life as a child. The big corn cribs with just-harvested corn cobs bursting out between the narrow slats, the horse collars hanging on horse stall walls, wagon wheels, wagon tongues, plow sweeps, parts for harrows and other farm machinery, hay wagons, and of course, all the animals and chickens. What fun it was!

Theodora also had memories of her paternal grandparents, Grandpa Frank and Grandma Ann DeGraaff.

The same family ritual of devotions was practiced there, but before the meal Grandpa always prayed the Lord's Prayer in the Dutch language, a precious memory. My parents followed the traditions of their parents, so I grew up with the Bible and prayer. I also prayed alongside my bed before bedtime with my parents listening.

My parents were raised on Bible memorization, and that was handed down to me, so the value of learning Saturday catechism and Sunday school memory verses was instilled in me. In the early primary grades, if you knew your weekly verse, you earned a pretty, small Bible card, so that was a good incentive and motivating. I was always ready to count and tell my grandparents how many verses I knew and cards I had earned. But we started early in the week and worked at it all week long.

Grandpa Frank was a self-taught Bible scholar. He would help me with my catechism lessons and writing out prayers. This was good. It taught me how to formulate my thoughts into prayers.

Such Bible memorization was a requirement for those of us raised in these strict Dutch homes with their strong Calvinist tradition. But those verses stayed with us, and both my cousin and I can attest to the hope they brought, especially in later years, when we were up against trying times and these comforting verses surfaced.

"THE HAND OF GOD IS ALWAYS OUTSTRETCHED"

We learned from our parents the importance of spiritual values. One of the things they impressed upon us was that the hand of God is always outstretched, ready to lift you up. Mom really knew the power of prayer. She had polio at six months, and it left her with a life-long disability, but she turned it into an ability that was a hallmark of her faith. She learned to walk at age three with the aid of braces. She never complained, was always thankful, and the Word of God was on her lips at all times. She had a wonderful sense of humor, the ability to laugh and make others laugh. Both Dad and Mother were towers of love, faith, and hope.

In the 1950s, after extensive knee surgery, she had to learn to walk again. She was never able to abandon the brace on her leg. It was painful and difficult, but she mastered it one step at a time. She would say, "I can do all things through Christ who strengthens me." She was our tower of strength when she needed support herself.

Even with her disability, she exemplified in her life the importance of doing little acts of kindness for others. One night I phoned and asked her how many visitors she'd had that day—there were 34 people who had dropped by. On one Father's Day weekend they had 96 callers. Mother and Dad shared in the lives of others—both the joys and sorrows. And you knew they would prepare and bring over a meal when there was a need. You could count on their love. I learned the meaning of love from my grandparents and parents.

My father was "a sermon in shoes," in living and giving, sharing and caring. He always counted God's blessings instead of hardships. I can still see Dad walking with our dear old neighbor, Grandpa Schaap, who would make his way to the corner of our block and wait for my dad. They had a set time to meet daily. Then the old grandpa would take my dad's arm and say, "Okay, Francis, let's really step" (which meant walk fast).

When our first child was born (I remember this like yesterday), my mom held her new first grandson and said, "Now, when you take this little son's booties off and later his shoes, always say a prayer to God for him. When I was born, someone gave a little poem to my mother, your grandmother, and she passed it on to me, and it meant a lot. Now I want you to pass this on to your own children someday when they present you with grandchildren:

> God has sent you from above
> a little soul for you to love,
> a tender gift to watch and keep,
> to love and kiss and croon to sleep.
> Happy parents proud and blest,
> may this tiny treasure rest,
> shielded from the world apart,
> in the haven of your heart."

It has become a cherished family tradition, as each of my own grandchildren were born, to pass it on to their parents.

Living in proximity to their children and grandchildren has afforded this family opportunities to attend open-house school functions, Vacation Bible School and Sunday school programs, Christmas and other holiday get-togethers and church programs, sporting events in which the grandchildren are participants, birthday parties, sleepovers, gardening, reading, fishing, camping, and other wonderful times of family togetherness that mean so much.

Theodora continued:

We helped the grandchildren memorize the names of the 66 books of the Bible, and then we played games with them to help them remember. When loving and cuddling them, I would whisper, "How are you doing spiritually?" and they knew what I meant.

One memory I am sure our grandchildren will not forget were the hours we spent playing "Little House on the Prairie"—Grandma Kracht's version, with lots of imagination. I brought out all the old shoes, dresses, and hats. We dressed up in the pioneer clothes and hats and then went down to our creek and had our "wagon train lunch." Wow! Fun for hours!

I am a working grandmother, and I have had the unique pleasure of employment in the newborn nursery at the Luverne, Minnesota, hospital. I cared for five of the seven grandchildren born into our family. I felt so close to God when I took each newborn child from the arms of his mother and put him on the scale to be weighed. There was a special bonding that took place in that moment between me, as grandmother, and this infant. I could only thank and praise God, pray and dedicate him to the Lord.

As I reflect on my upbringing and on the way my parents were raised by their parents, my grandparents, and now on the way my husband and I raised our children and how these children are raising their children, our grandchildren, I see a continuity that has been handed down from one generation to another. We were taught principles of right and wrong, values, how to trust and obey, how to be respectful of others, and to seek wisdom. We were taught to succeed, to do the best you could, where you were, with what you had. Often, when facing hard times, one or the other of my parents would say, "The Lord is our shepherd, we shall not want" (quoting from the much-loved favorite, Psalm 23).

We were taught to accept a challenge, given food for thought by suggestions and words of encouragement from parents and grandparents, and always to reach out to God in prayer.

Mom and Dad believed in us when sometimes we had trouble believing in ourselves. They never let on to us when we disappointed them. They knew when we needed their silence more than words. Their godly wisdom was wonderful.

There was sound teaching about the need to learn forgiveness. "If someone has done you a wrong, forgive," my mother would say. "Sometimes forgiveness is even the best revenge," and we knew the Scripture: " 'Vengeance is mine,' saith the Lord." And she would say, "Forgiveness is not necessarily for the sake of others as much as for your own sake. We all need to learn to forgive if we are to be forgiven by God."

Teachings such as this came from hearts of wisdom. Cousin Maggie's parents had made known the truths of God's Word to their daughter, she had absorbed them into the very fiber of her being, and it was as natural as breathing for her to pass on what she knew to be Truth.

The challenge for grandparents today is great—our grandchildren face peer pressure, and the lures of the world are ever present. Parents and grandparents must exercise patience as they walk through these challenges with their loved ones. My constant prayer is *Dear God, help me to be a reflection of You.*

While this cousin's parents were still living, and during her father's retirement years, they cut out quilt squares. The entire family—all the children and grandchildren—worked at this together.

As we did, we reminisced, sharing the good memories. It was a super-fun day. Later, we sewed the pieces together. (My sister and sister-in-law brought their sewing machines over to our mother's house.) I pressed and pressed the pieces, then we had to cut out some more, and Mom was right there, helping everywhere. We had potluck, fun, and fellowship while we worked at this. Today we all have beautiful quilts, a reminder of a very special time for everyone.

"MY LIFE'S CANDLE FLAME"

Theodora's son Carl also wrote an essay for school, which he entitled "My Life's Candle Flame":

The lives of my grandparents are good examples of the benefits of a tremendous faith in God and a positive attitude for each new day. They are people whose lives are a shining example of counting blessings instead of hardships. Their lives have proven that happiness depends upon where one's confidence lies. They cannot always control their circumstances, but they do have a choice of attitudes in every situation.

My grandmother is truly an example of courage and enthusiasm to all who know her. She has suffered from polio since the age of six months. She has undergone a series of surgeries on her polio leg. The operations were unsuccessful. She had been using braces to walk, but for the last 20 years she has been confined to a wheelchair. Throughout these experiences, she has never lost her optimistic outlook on life, her deep faith in God, or her self-esteem. If you were ever to meet this wonderful example of mine, you would never forget her. She leaves everyone with a sense of accomplishment and awe.

My grandfather had many fine qualities; among those were his honesty and willingness to work. He taught me to be content with what I have. Grandfather would go out of his way to make those around him happy. If he thought someone was in dire need, he would go without and give the other person whatever was needed. The little things in life counted highly, and to my grandfather this rule was never taken for granted. A cheery "hello" and a smile brightened the days for the people with whom he worked.

One event my grandfather especially enjoyed was Christmas. He played Santa Claus to thousands of children in his lifetime, and he was eventually made the official Santa Claus in the town of Hull, Iowa. When Grandfather played Santa Claus, he was love dressed in red and white. Santa Claus is charity, goodwill toward men, and a parallel symbol of God's love and might. That was also what my grandfather was all about. He treated everyone as though it was Christmas year 'round.

When cancer took control of his body, that didn't keep him from thinking of others. His main concern was that the family stay together. With God's help, we have remained and will continue to be together. Although Grandfather has passed on, his contributions live on through the lives of others. His son (my uncle) and I continue playing Santa Claus to children. I was honored to receive Grandfather's first Santa Claus suit and spread love and happiness as he did.

I owe a lot to these two fine people. They encouraged me to succeed in whatever I set out to do, and to do it to the best of my ability. My grandparents are two of the finest examples of contentment and happiness you will ever find.

If ever the world needed active and effective grandparents, it's now. If it seems like I'm asking grandparents to be superpeople, I am. Grandparents should ask no less of themselves.

—ARTHUR KORNHABER, M.D., IN *VITAL CONNECTIONS*

14

GRANDCHILDREN AND DEATH

Jesus said to her [Martha], "I am the resurrection and the life;
he who believes in Me will live even if he dies, and everyone
who lives and believes in Me shall never die."
—JOHN 11:25-26 (NASB)

A five-year-old, spending the night with his grandparents, was praying the prayer generations of children have prayed: "Now I lay me down to sleep. I pray the Lord my soul to keep. If I should die before I wake..." He paused. "Grandma," he said, "I don't want to pray my dead prayer anymore." Grandma was momentarily tipped off balance!

Everyone wants to go to heaven, but no one wants to die. Like the little guy, we back away from the idea of death. "Death is the supreme enigma ... the great interrupter ... the last thing we talk about ... a terrible enemy even for one with faith in God, because the Enemy has not yet been destroyed." So wrote Joe Bayly.[1] If anyone knew what he was talking about regarding death, it was Joe, for three of his sons were "carried home to heaven by the angels." He could write this with certainty because he believed Jesus' words (e.g., Luke 16:22). We speak of it as loss, for that's certainly what it is for those of us left on this side of heaven, but for our loved ones, we can have the assurance that it is gain.[2] Yet we are so very human: We don't want our loved ones in heaven yet; we want them with us.

GRADUATION TO GLORY

When death claimed my mother, I saw something precious in my son Kraig, who was six years old at the time. It was the reality of faith. He understood the moment he saw Grandma Hattie lying in the coffin that death was real, but so was life everlasting. The evening we went to the funeral home, I tried to prepare the children for the experience. I told them that if they wanted to touch her hand, they could, but that it wouldn't be the warm, soft hand they were accustomed to holding. Kraig and his Grandma had spent endless hours with each other. She was a widow, so she and I were very close. She had never remarried, and after I married, she lived near us and spent a lot of time with us. She baby-sat often, and the children dearly loved their Grandma Hattie. Because Kraig was the youngest grandchild, he'd spent more time with her in her later years. She'd played games with him, encouraged him in his drawing, and read to him. They did everything together.

Kraig, who adored his Grandma, walked into the room at the

mortuary, a brave little guy. He laid his head on the side of the casket, just as he had in the convalescent home at her bedside. He looked at her dear face for a long, long while. Then, shyly, he reached over and touched her hand. One final long look, a deep sigh, and he looked up at me, tears in his eyes, then turned and looked around at everyone, and very clearly so all could hear, he announced, "No, she's not there. That's just her shell. My Grandma's in heaven with Jesus." There wasn't a dry eye in the room. That little boy had just given the message that has stayed with all of us ever since—death is real, but so is heaven.

We could smile through our tears, even as Grandma's boy was doing. And I had the most awesome feeling that my mother was seeing this also. We knew that to be "away from the body" was to be "at home with the Lord" (2 Corinthians 5:8), but Kraig's words brought the reality home to us. Yes, Grandma Hattie was still living. She was with her Lord in her heavenly home. Grandma had graduated to glory.

GRANDCHILDREN AND THE DEATH EXPERIENCE

Since that experience, I, as a grandmother, have walked through the death experience with my own children and grandchildren five times. They have lost all of their grandparents and great-grandparents on both sides, except for me. I have found it comforting to think that none of these dear departed loved ones was *sent* into the "valley of the shadow of death" (Psalm 23:4), but rather they were taken *through* it, led by the Good Shepherd right on into eternal life. Sharing this with grandchildren is a comfort.

Today, at many memorial services (or "celebrations," as so many of us like to call them), friends and family members give tributes. This is touching, though for some, much as they would like to share, they are pretty certain they couldn't do it without losing their composure. But it is comforting to the bereaved as others relate their experiences and what they will especially remember about a loved one. Many such tributes were given at my husband's service, and I was touched and comforted by every sentiment expressed. I remember Dustin, our 16-year-old grandson, lovingly reminiscing about Grandpa Herman.

Martin R. De Haan II—grandson of Dr. M. R. De Haan, founder of the Radio Bible Class ministry—wrote movingly about his beloved grandfather in the *Discovery Digest "Grandparents and Grandchildren"* booklet, a contribution entitled "The Legacy." He talked about Grandpa De Haan's beehives, fishing trips, birdhouses, huge yard, and love of nature. He

---

Maybe today or tomorrow or one day soon we will hear the shout of the archangel. Christ will return. We will be caught up to be with the Lord, who first saved our grandparents, then our parents, and then us. ... Perhaps today, the real legacy—the legacy of grandparents who loved God and looked eagerly for the return of the Lord—will be realized. —MARTIN R. DE HAAN II, GRANDSON OF DR. M. R. DE HAAN, FOUNDER OF THE RADIO BIBLE CLASS MINISTRY

---

shared memories of his Grandpa's barn, his study, his jokes, his hunting stories, and his bristly kisses. "But the memories that are the most important are those that have continued to grow in importance: the spiritual memories, his love for the Word of God, his passion for the salvation of lost people—"

Martin talked also about his beloved grandma and concluded:

We sense that their work is not done. The legacy goes on. Grandpa was not just a gardener and a fisherman. He planted the Word of God in the hearts of millions. He fished for men. He proved over and over what the Scriptures teach.[3]

The scriptures Martin De Haan referred to in "The Legacy":

- The quality of a person's life affects his children for generations to come (Exodus 34:7).
- Each generation makes its own choices about what it will do with its inheritance (Genesis 25:27-34; Ezekiel 18).
- A generation's honor is seen in what it leaves for those who follow (Proverbs 13:22).

"FOR THEY SHALL BE COMFORTED"

There are two sides to death: a dark side and a bright side. The dark side is experienced by those left behind and certainly not the ones who have departed to be with the Lord. When we are going through the loss of a loved one, however, it is hard to think of the bright side—the thought of separation intrudes. We are faced with the loss of companionship. The apostle Paul told us to comfort one another with the blessed hope that one day we will be reunited (1 Thessalonians 4:13-18). Talk about these verses with grieving grandchildren, and point out the bright side of death.

Never forget that when we ourselves are grieving and walking through this heartbreak, so are our grandchildren. Decisions have to be made, many things have to be taken care of, and all the while the dear others in our life are grieving. This is unspeakably difficult. But while they need us, we need them. We reach for each other in our silent grief. And tears will flow.

Remember: Jesus wept! And it was at Lazarus's death (John 11:35). Dr. Billy Graham spoke at the memorial service for Dr. V. Raymond Edman, chancellor of Wheaton College, Wheaton, Illinois, in 1967, quoting something he'd heard Dr. Edman speak about years before. "None of us can escape death. There is a day, an hour, and a minute when our moment will come. Life is very brief: a tale that is told, a weaver's shuttle, a flower that fades, grass that withers."[4]

The truth is that it is not death to die. Our souls live on, freed from the bodies that held them. Death, for the Christian, is the passageway to glory.

CELEBRATING THE JOY OF HEAVEN

When my husband preceded me in death, I found it difficult to accept the fact that now I was the matriarch in the family. I thought, *It can't be. I'm not ready.* Death often finds the generations moving up a notch.

While writing this, my daughter and I were remembering my husband's sudden death (we called it his immediate translation into heaven). He would have said, "Hey! What a way to go!" The sting of death was removed when we concentrated on the joy Herman was experiencing. Indeed, ever since he came to the Lord as the runaway boy, he'd lived with his eye fixed on the goal of someday being with the Lord. We kept our focus on the celebration God had for him upon his arrival. And that made it possible for us to celebrate too.

Martha Ashworth speaks with joy recalling how she helped her grandchildren remember their "Pa Pa's having gone to heaven" on the first Father's Day after his death. They made the memory a celebration.

> We expected it would be a difficult day. Five of the grandchildren and two of my children were nearby. I asked each grandchild to write a message of whatever they'd like to tell Pa Pa in heaven. We went to the cemetery, where each child attached his or her special message and pictures to a balloon.... They released their balloons... to heaven to be read by Pa Pa. I then presented each grandchild with a new Bible with their names....We then read a poem entitled "Hi, Granddad" and said a special prayer. As we left for church, we ... were full of smiles and laughter. What could have been a day of sad memories became one of fun and joy.

T. W. Wilson's granddaughter Christy Kurpier gave a tribute at her grandfather's memorial celebration. She entitled it "My Granddaddy."

When I think of my granddaddy, there are so many things that I cherish. I think of a house filled with warm laughter as he shared stories after dinner....

I think of us wrestling on the floor as he never tired of playing horsey with me.

I think of his eyes as he taught me how to wink and to belly-laugh when I finally did.

I think of the wisdom and direction he gave me in my time of need.

I think of the night before Christmas as he read from the Bible every year as our family gathered.

I think of his hands outstretched to say, "I love you very much"—each finger representing our secret code....

I think of the words he said to encourage me to pursue my dreams....

I think of the pride I feel in the heritage that courses through my veins.

Mostly, though, I think of love—an unconditional love that defies any description.

Granddaddy makes me want to be the person that he always said he saw in me. And for that I will love him and carry a piece of him with me always.

I love you very much, Granddaddy.

THE DIFFICULT "FIRSTS"

Phyllis Seminoff wrote about the death of her husband in February 2000 and how she knew it was a must that something be done to keep her family strong at Christmas. The first holidays following the loss of a loved one are especially difficult. Phyllis wrote:

> One afternoon in May, as Granddaughter Emily and I were thinking ahead to the holidays, we came up with the idea of entertaining the family Christmas Eve with a meaningful Christmas play. On another day, as she and I got further into the writing of the play, she remarked, "Grammy, I wish we could do the play for other people too, like in a nursing home or whatever." As I thought about my grandchild wanting to share the message of Christmas with others, the library I was coordinating for our church came to mind. At some point I desired to do a benefit where families could "gift" books to the children's portion of the library and have fun doing it. Putting on the Christmas play seemed the right thing. This would serve a dual purpose—it would benefit the children's library while giving the Seminoffs' Christmas family togetherness at its best.

Consulting with the children's ministries of New Hope Christian Fellowship in Vacaville, California, and suggesting they combine the library event with the children's annual Christmas program and party were the first steps. The leadership of the church enthusiastically agreed.

What an opportunity this could be to reach out to children, parents, and the community. After two months of rehearsals and much dedication from all involved, on the day of the performance all went off without a hitch. Many hearts were touched and two hundred–plus books, videos, cassettes, and CDs were gifted to the children's library. New relationships were formed to be treasured, and the children and adults had a part in reaching out to others. And precious to me, our family stayed close through that difficult first Christmas without my husband and the children's dearly loved Grandpa Bill. For our children and grandchildren, I believe, a lasting memory was formed. I know that working together as a unit, doing the work of the Lord, is something they will always remember and value.

I saw that library and what a great gift it is to that church and community. Emily got her wish to present the Christmas play not only to the church but also to a nursing home and retirement center in that community. Quietly, in her lovely, self-effacing way, Phyllis says, "Living one's life for the glory of God sets people apart. We *must* pass on our legacy of faith to our families."

THE UNTHINKABLE

"Who ever thinks that one of their children will precede them in death?" This was just one of the responses I heard from grandparents having walked through the death experience with grandchildren after a mother or father had gone ahead to be with the Lord. These grandparents had gone through "the unthinkable."

Bill and Marilyn Barnard of Dallas, Texas, found themselves crying out, wanting answers as they watched the life of their beautiful daughter Linda slowly ebb away. *"God, she is so young, so lovely, such a radiant Christian. Her husband and children need her. We need her; we can't bear losing her.... God, spare her, heal her."* The Barnards speak with gratitude for the loving ministrations of one of their daughter's friends, Sarah Lee Parrish, who came to be with Linda and helped care for the children during each of Linda's five chemotherapy treatments. But the day came when Linda held her one-and-a-half-year-old old son on her lap for the last time and tenderly gave her last hug to four-year-old Emily. She looked into the eyes of her husband and parents, and then she was gone.

"Man is destined to die once," the writer of Hebrews tells us. "Birth and death enclose man in a sort of parenthesis of the present," says Joe Bayly. "And the brackets at the beginning and end of life are still impenetrable."[5]

God supplied the strength for Bill and Marilyn on a moment-by-moment basis. Marilyn stayed behind in Illinois to care for the two young children and offer help to her son-in-law. Bill, taking time off from his work at Dallas Theological Seminary, flew up to be with all of them. Their son-in-law's mother also flew in from South Carolina. In this way, the two grandmothers were there for the grandchildren during the initial adjustment time.

How do grandparents walk through the death experience

with grandchildren? In this and other practical ways, doing the near-at-hand things to bring order and stability into a situation that has been so disrupted by loss, all the while leaning on God's promises and relying on His grace. "My grace is sufficient for you, for my power is made perfect in weakness" (2 Corinthians 12:9).

Neither Bill nor Marilyn felt very strong, but they held on to the reality that God was in this with them, that He would see them through. And He did. Not many months later, their son-in-law moved to South Carolina, where his family helped in the care of his children. Still later, he married again, but he has remained close to the Barnards, allowing them the joy of participating in the growing-up days of their precious grandchildren.

Both grandmothers helped little Emily, who was just old enough to understand that her mommy was in heaven with Jesus and that someday she would get to see her again and be with her for all eternity.

Regardless of one's age, I am convinced that the death of a child is the most unnatural and hardest of deaths to bear. God doesn't turn away from honesty and the crying out and questioning that accompany this kind of loss. "Time heals wounds," goes the old truism, yet we know that it is God who uses time for His purposes. In God's time, we can come to grips with what has happened.

THE UNEXPLAINABLE

At times, the meaning of life seemed far removed from Bill and Marilyn. They found comfort in their understanding of God's sovereignty. "God doesn't make mistakes," Bill said in a conversation. This is the point at which they were able to get some answers to their questioning cries. Everyone at one time or another asks the "Why?" question. Eventually, their "whys" became "what?" *"What, God, can we do with this pain to bring glory to You?"*

God is a God of love. Lamentations 3:33 says that God does not willingly afflict the children of men. It gives the heavenly Father no pleasure to see His children suffer. God allowed His only Son to suffer and die a cruel death for us. But even recognizing all this, the grief is never entirely muted.

The pain is still there in Bill and Marilyn's eyes. But there is also a glint of serene acceptance. "God took us through," Bill quietly said.

"When you pass through the waters, I will be with you; And through the rivers, they shall not overflow you. When you walk through the fire, you shall not be burned.... For I am the Lord your God" (Isaiah 43:2, 3a, NKJV).

As Joe Bayly's eight-year-old daughter said, "[When someone dies] it's like something is pinned to the front of your mind all the time."[6] There are no easy answers to pain, suffering, and death. But we who ask the questions are in good company with Job, Moses, and hosts of others throughout the centuries, right up to the present moment, who cried out with grief and sadness and experienced God's comforting grace.

C. S. Lewis experienced the loss of his wife, whom he had married in midlife. His odyssey of grief is recorded in *A Grief Observed.* He had intense moments of clarity in the depths of his horrible experience: "Grief is like a long valley, a winding valley where any bend may reveal a totally new landscape."[7]

The loss of one's children is surely one of the cruelest of pains, certain to rouse a person wherever he finds himself on the continuum of life. Our Christian faith doesn't promise us immunity from this or any other kind of pain, but our faith does enable us to accept and come through it. Job, who lost all his children, was able to raise a boil-encrusted arm and cry out, "Though he slay me, yet will I hope in him" (Job 13:15). It is this kind of acceptance and trust we can give to our precious grandchildren.

To our grandchildren, we can show that we accept life's mysteries and sufferings unexplained. God knows and He has a plan (Jeremiah 29:11). His ways are beyond explaining (Isaiah 55:9, Romans 11:33-36). To try and reason our way through these dark times, these crises of faith, is "a deceptively weak crutch for faith. Reason gropes in the dark for answers, while faith waits for God."[8]

SUICIDE AND A GRANDMOTHER'S EXAMPLE

One of the most traumatic and hurtful experiences loved ones can endure is suicide. This is not the place for me to try and write in detail about that. I have written a book entitled *A Time to Speak* (soon to be published) in which I discuss this. Suffice here to say that a grandparent whose grandchild takes his or her own life, or a son or daughter who commits suicide leaving grandchildren to console and help, are left with the kind of pain that is all but indescribable.

Vicki Bohe-Thackwell, co-author of *A Time to Speak,* went through this experience at age 21 when her mother took her own life. I asked her to comment.

It was a tragic loss for my family and for my grandparents. We all mourned for a long while. Two years after my mother's death, I visited my grandmother. I saw the way my grandmother gave her suffering to God daily. I saw the sadness in her eyes, but I also saw something else. I saw strength. Once again she gave me a spiritual gift. She gave me a way to deal with my grief by bringing Jesus into the grieving process.

EXPLAINING DEATH TO A YOUNG CHILD

Doris Sanford, author of the *Hurts of Childhood* book series, says that "grief is not a problem to be cured. It is simply a statement that you loved somebody." She points out that children are often forgotten in times of grief but that death *is* an issue for them and that, in a survey of children ages 8 to 14, they said that their greatest fear was "that my parents might die."

To explain death to a young child, always respond on the maturity level of the child. As you help him through the grieving process:

• Tell the child the truth about what happened, simply and lovingly. Answer questions in a brief way. When my mother died, we explained to the children that the "real" grandma was gone, and Kraig's ability to process this showed in his statement that it was "Grandma's shell" that was left, that Grandma was in heaven with God. It's a good idea to talk to the children about this if they are taken in to see the loved one's body.

• Understand that children, like adults, will ask the "Why?" question too. Use scriptures; some are included in this chapter. Tell the children that the Bible says, "The secret things belong to the LORD our God, but the things revealed belong to us and to our children forever" (Deuteronomy 29:29). I told the grand-children that we don't have to live down here on earth forever, that we get to go to heaven, which is far better. Heaven is a beautiful place. Show them the scriptures that describe it. Explain that we don't have all the answers to the "Why?" ques-tion, but the answers are hidden in the heart of God, and we can just "tuck them away on the shelf of faith" for now. We comfort ourselves with the knowledge that God never makes mistakes or allows a useless or wrongly timed act. If our minds were as wide as the mind of God, and if we were where He is, we would understand. Romans 8:28 says, "And *we know* that in all things God works for the good of those who love him" (emphasis added). It doesn't say, "we hope so" or "maybe" or "might be." This is a "know-so" reality.[9]

• Tell the child that it's okay to feel sad and to cry. Explain that even Jesus wept when He learned of His friend Lazarus's death. You may need to explain what's going on when the child sees others grieve. "We're going to miss Grandma, and it helps to cry. The Bible says our tears are precious to God."

• Tiny people need to feel the loving arms of a caring adult who tells them, "I love you. I understand how you feel. It hurts, but I'm here to help you." Bill and Marilyn's four-year-old granddaughter, Emily, would tell her grandma, "I feel sad. I want my mama." And Marilyn would tenderly hug and comfort her. Marilyn's other daughter had fixed scrapbooks with pictures, cards, and mementos for her niece and nephew, and Marilyn would bring those out and together they would look at them.

• There is no timetable for grief recovery in either adults or children. Much depends on how close the child was to the one who died. If the departed was sick for some time, it is good to let the child know that this was expected. Preparing the child in advance for this can help. If the death was sudden and unexpected, it may be more difficult and take longer for the child to adjust. The support that surrounds the child is of critical importance in helping the child to bear the loss. It's healthy to encourage the child to talk about what he or she remembers about the grandparent (or whomever), and it can provide occasions for them to laugh as they recall Grandpa's silly jokes, his loving nature, or kind things he did. Encourage such open sharing among family members. Allow the child to see that the loved one lives on in your hearts.

• If the death occurs during the school year, inform the child's teacher that the child is facing a major life change. Also inform parents of a child's friends so they can explain to their children.

• Watch for poor school performance. Also, watch for physical symptoms, such as stomachaches, headaches, fatigue, and depression. You may see misbehavior or hear self-deprecating remarks, such as "Nobody likes me" or "I'm stupid." Encourage the child to express his feelings, but correct any negative, misdirected grief. He may be internalizing his feelings and need help in going through the grief process. He may have fear, and he needs to understand that one death doesn't mean more are on the way. Children need safe times, safe places, and safe people in their young lives. They can be shown that God is their safety at all times, but you can be "God with a face" for them. Remember, grandparents represent stability.

• Pray with the child. Assure him that God listens to his prayers and that it's okay to talk about one's fears, heartache, sadness, and even anger with God. Pray with the child and remind him that you are praying for him, just as many others are. Give him your favorite verses on prayer (you might want to print them out for him). Remind your grandchild that God says, "Call to me and I will answer you" (Jeremiah 33:3).

• Treat your grandchild to a fun time. Give him some choices; ask what he'd like to do or see. Maybe splurge on a new toy. Take him out to eat. Give of yourself to create a pleasant memory.

These are just some of the ways you can help a child work through grief. And, of course, above all, hug.

GRANDPA NATE'S SACRIFICE

In July 2000, Marj Saint VanDerPuy's 20-year-old granddaughter, Stephenie, died of a brain aneurysm. This sudden, unexpected tragedy happened on the eve of her father Steve's departure for the Billy Graham Amsterdam 2000 Evangelism Conference.

For those unfamiliar with Steve Saint's story, Nate Saint was a pilot for the Missionary Aviation Fellowship (MAF) in 1956, and one of the five men killed in the jungles of Ecuador by warriors from the Auca tribe (now known as the Waodoni). Two and a half years later, Steve's Aunt Rachel Saint entered the tribe where she ministered and translated the Bible until her death in 1994. Steve visited her often and came to love the Waodani, and so it was that he brought his wife and children to the heart of the Amazon to serve the very tribe that killed his father. The full account is given in Steve's excellent book, *The Great Omission* (YWAM Publishing, 2001).

Thus it was at the July 2000 conference, that Steve introduced two men from the Waodani tribe of Ecuador, who shared of having become Christians because of the witness of Steve's aunt, Rachel Saint, and Steve and his family. Steve introduced Mincaye as "grandfather" to his children, and who today was mourning the loss of his only blonde granddaughter.

"We both loved her very much," Steve explained. "I told the delegates that Mincaye had killed my children's own grandfather before he learned to walk 'God's trail.' "

Ten years after the death of her first husband, Nate, Marj was remarried to Abe VanDerPuy in Quito, Ecuador. It's a beautiful story of how God moved in their lives, Abe becoming the father for Marj's children that they needed, and Marj becoming mother to Abe's children. The loss of their granddaughter was a heartrending experience, made bearable by the knowledge that Stephenie was with the Lord.[10]

Five months later, at 3:30 on Christmas morning, Steve Saint wrote the following. When I told Marj about the book I was writing, she sent this, feeling it might belong here. When you read it, I think you will agree that it does.

Lonely, Lovely Christmas

This Christmas, as the world around me glitters with tinsel and lights, my heart screams out its loneliness. Our beautiful daughter is not here—how can there be a celebration?

What significance can there be in gifts and carols when that happy, bouncing little girl with pigtails— grown up to be our stately and beautiful daughter—is not here to sing with us? Every tradition of sound and smell that makes this season jolly reminds me that my heart has been rent.

This Christmas I am still safe and warm, but my heart feels the icy blasts. My soul is locked out in the cold while my mind tries to make merry inside. What can redeem this Christmas for a brokenhearted father? Only the return of my precious child.

I finally begin to grasp a reality of this season. It took a Father's broken heart to make my place at the Great Celebration. That same Father spent the first Christmas without His Child to buy me a spot at His banquet table. With His grief, He has enfolded my little girl in eternal love. By His agony, I will see my precious little girl again and my heart will be healed.

I can finally feel the icy fingers that stab at that other Daddy's heart. Many of His children are still lost in the cold. What a terrible pain it has taken to make me feel the hurt He bore to bring us warm inside.

A GRANDFATHER'S PRAYER

The testimony, prayer, and final wishes of John Heusinkveld, a dear father and grandfather, dated March 28, 1957, express his love for his descendants and the Lord. Up until his dying day, John looked for the "blessed hope": the coming of the Lord Jesus Christ. He wrote out his favorite scriptures, the songs he wanted sung, and burial instructions, making it easier for his loved ones to carry out his wishes. He was a saint, a dear, elderly gentleman, whom Herman and I got to know when we lived in Sunnyvale, California. His final written words were "I want to see and meet you all in the morning when Jesus comes for His own." It was signed: "Your Father and Grandfather."

We will do our families an immense favor if we are as thoughtful as John was to his. It is a good thing for us to take time and think through our memorial service. To write our love for dear ones we cherish, to assure them that we are in heaven with the Lord (and with others gone before us), is to give them hope and foresight for their own day of departure. Death is but the stepping-stone to eternity. Yet through echoing our grandchildren's prayers, we can live each day until then gloriously for our heavenly Father.

As I come to the conclusion of this chapter, one in which I could say so much more, I am reminded of the prayer of one of my grandchildren many years ago. I wrote it down and redis-covered it in the material I had filed to use in writing this chap-ter. This darling little one had prayed, "Thank You, God, for not having us die ..." I remember she had paused, and then added, "... yet."

That grandchild is now a beautiful young lady making her way in a fast-changing world, a world that in many respects her progenitors would barely recognize. But they would be proud of her, proud and thankful. The legacy of faith they passed on is alive and well in this young woman, her sister, her brother, and her cousins.

"When the Son of Man returns, will He find faith on the earth?" Were You to come tomorrow, Lord, we could answer truthfully, *"Yes, Lord."*

15

RESPONDING TO CRISES

When you pass through the waters, I will be with you;
And through the rivers, they shall not overflow you.
When you walk through the fire, you shall not be burned,
Nor shall the flame scorch you.
For I am the Lord your God,
The Holy One of Israel, your Savior.
—ISAIAH 43:2-3 (NKJV)

One grandmother told of overhearing her four-year-old grandson lean over his whimpering, year-old brother and ask, "What's your problem?"

A good question! These precious little ones do pick up on what they hear adults say, don't they?

Jesus told His followers that here on earth they would encounter many problems and sorrows. When these trials invade our lives, however, we cry out for answers. The inequities of life, the things that seem unfair—we find ourselves stumbling through the maze of fear, questions, hurt, anger, disbelief, and even rage. We wrestle with the age-old question: If God is a God of love and mercy, why do righteous people suffer?

From our vantage point of maturity and experience, how do we help our children and grandchildren through the maze of crisis times?

This is no place for pat answers, but I hold firmly to God's sovereignty and trustworthiness. In circumstances beyond my control, and in times of crisis and uncertainty, I lean heavily on my faith, but also on my trust.

Dr. James Dobson says, "I'm convinced that faith in moments of crisis is insufficient, unless we are also willing to trust our very lives to His care."[1] That is so important. My grandchildren have heard me say many times, "You can trust yourself to the God who made you for He will never fail you." Then I tell them that's what the apostle Peter said (paraphrased from 1 Peter 4:19).

Even while writing the last few chapters of this book, I was experiencing a crisis of excruciating back pain as a result of an accident that seemed so senseless and kept me from staying on schedule with this manuscript. While I was no stranger to pain and the attempts of the Enemy to thwart our plans, a broken back can sap your energy very quickly. My temptation was to succumb to disillusionment and make "if only…" statements.

But during that time, favorite passages and the words of beloved old hymns came back to me, filling my thoughts. I was also greatly helped by Dr. Dobson's book *When God Doesn't Make Sense.* I would urge anyone dealing with a crisis to read his book and let its message sink in. In it, Dr. Dobson says, "God will always be the determiner of what is best for those who serve Him."[2] I can certainly attest to that.

WHEN THE BIG "C" INVADES OUR LIVES

Recently, my friend Carita and her daughter and granddaughters found themselves living through the "most difficult months" of their lives. As Carita expressed it:

> ...I feel like I've aged five years. My dear precious
> daughter, Elizabeth, has cancer, a malignant brain
> tumor. Even as I write this, it seems unreal. I've been
> gone day and night. We take turns being with Elizabeth
> and her three children at her home, and when I'm not
> there, I'm doing research on the Internet....
>
> We are truly taking it one day at a time....

I knew what she was going through. We had been down that road as a family when my 16-year-old grandson was diagnosed with cancer in his left leg, shortly before Christmas in 1995. I still feel the wrenching pain of that moment of discovery and diagnosis. Wrapping my arms around him, I committed him to God's loving care. "God is in this with you, Dustin."

It had only been eight months since my husband died; we were all still feeling *that* loss. My own fears and tears were close to the surface. Today, Dustin walks with a limp, but he *can* walk

229

and he still has his leg. For many months and many surgeries we weren't sure what the outcome would be.

Hospitalization. Tests. Biopsy. Our worst fears were confirmed. When told that he had a rare form of bone cancer, osteogenic sarcoma, Dustin cried out, "Mom, I don't want to die!"

My daughter's heart broke. "What could I say?" she recounted. "I found myself reminding him that he had a heavenly Father who loved him very much and that He had a plan and we had to trust Him." The surgeon had told my daughter that it was a "stage-four" cancer—the most aggressive kind there is—and that treatment needed to begin at once.

So Dustin went into limb salvage surgery, well aware that he might come out without his leg. It was a long surgery, but enough bone was salvageable so that a titanium bar could be inserted. He received his first intravenous chemotherapy drip on his 17th birthday in the cancer ward at the Kaiser Hospital in Sacramento. Balloons, tied to his bed by long strings, bumped against the ceiling. The doctor had decided that friends could celebrate the big day in his room. *How many more birthdays will my grandson have?* I wondered, walking into his hospital room that night.

Dustin spent most of that year in the hospital cancer ward. There were six more surgeries and extensive physical therapy in conjunction with the aggressive chemotherapy program which had to be stopped after he received his lifetime limit. There were times when we all felt the Lord's presence, sensing ministering angels surrounding the bed. My daughter never left his side during his hospital stays. She had opportunities to speak to parents and patients, sharing the strong faith supporting her and Dustin. The doctors and nurses found his room was "just different from other rooms." They said Dustin's faith and the faith of family members were creating an atmosphere for healing. Faith was being tested, and we were to emerge stronger, wiser, humbler, more certain than ever of God's care. God's Word was the stronghold, the armor that warded off the Enemy's attacks.

God doesn't take us into deep water to drown us. And He's not an arsonist, setting fires for the fun of it. The will of God will never take you where His love and grace cannot keep you. A scripture that saw me through many crisis times is Isaiah 26:3-4. I printed it out for Dustin.

> You will keep him in perfect peace
> Whose mind is stayed on you,
> Because he trusts in You.
> Trust in the LORD forever,
> For in YAH, the LORD, is everlasting strength.

"Let's keep ourselves God-focused, I said. And we did. His peace was there for us. We were buoyed through the difficult days, the long freeway trips, and Dustin being hooked to tubes as we shared with each other the discoveries we were making each on our own. My grandson was able to continue his education at home through a program with his school, and he graduated with his class in the spring of 1997.

Today, as I write this, my grandson has gone beyond the five years considered crucial in cancer recovery. God has been gracious and merciful. People were praying across the country. Their prayers were answered. Dustin's parents, Rhonda and Mike, went through the agonies of uncertainty fully confident that God was in control. His sisters, Leah and Christa, encouraged Dustin all along the way, praying and trusting, sustained by God. Each of these three grandchildren today has a strong testimony. When Dustin shares at youth outreach functions, students rise to their feet cheering and praising God.

ELIZABETH'S STORY

In the days that followed her daughter Elizabeth's diagnosis of "anaplastic astrocytoma" and her craniotomy, Carita's e-mails were painfully honest, showing the state of shock into which her family was so suddenly catapulted. Beginning on March 4, 2000, the trail of correspondence revealed a grandmother struggling through this ordeal with her daughter, her three little girls, and the rest of her family. The granddaughters could not be shielded, much as their grandmother would like to have spared them. When little two-year-old Sierra wanted to see where the craniotomy had been performed, Carita was there. Gently touching her mother's head, Sierra looked at her Mommy, then at her Grammie, and said, "It's a boo-boo owie." And, indeed, it was!

What follows is Elizabeth's story told through Carita's eyes:

March 16, 2000: With a lot of prayerful consideration and discussion among family members, Elizabeth decided she did not want to know a prognosis. We are not filling our minds with any limitations, only hopefulness. The doctor said radiation was the protocol for treatment. We left the doctor's consultation with a sense of strength, one wherein love, hope, faith, and determination will see Elizabeth (and all of us) through this ordeal. The journey has just begun. As Elizabeth said, "I have to survive to tuck my girls in at night and to see them grow up."...

March 22: Elizabeth's spirit remains strong; her faith even stronger. Radiation will last about seven to seven and a half weeks.... Chemo was talked about yesterday also. We move on in a sort of daze doing what we have to do....

We are seeking an M.D. who will oversee her nutritional and alternative healing methods (supplements, diet, etc.) as she pursues the conventional route as well.... Our number-one request is that you continue your personal prayers and renew your prayer chains.... Remember her for the 10 minutes or so that she's in radiation each day....

March 26: We hear repeatedly from four doctors.... We leave these appointments rather upbeat, believe it or not, still going strong on hope.

Elizabeth had a lengthy telephone conversation with a renowned brain surgeon from southern California—a friend of my stepson. He was extremely optimistic and helpful, advising that Elizabeth thoroughly and prayerfully decide on the path she wants to take. He concurred that prayer, relaxation, nutrition, diet, and attitude are important and that she's doing all the right things....

April 21: To our wonderful friends, we wish you a blessed Easter. Today ends Elizabeth's first week of radiation. The first three days weren't easy for her. We appreciate all of you who are sending thoughts and prayers during this difficult treatment time....

We have our good days and our not-so-good days, sad times and happy times. This is a lot to deal with, and keeping a household running with three children is plenty in itself. We caregivers try to relieve Elizabeth of most duties, and I'd say the routine is going well.

Take time to smell the roses! Life is precious, and it's all those little, so-called insignificant things that are ultimately very important. I don't mean to sound preachy, but my heart is filled with so much emotion. I'm thankful for each one of you. You are touching our hearts in ever so many ways.

Carita's list of e-mail recipients numbered well over a hundred. "[Our friends' e-mails] are so uplifting," she wrote. "I thank God for the computer, because it has been my therapy. To get encouragement from so many of you either early in the morning or at night when I come home keeps me going."

Crucial to all that was taking place was the way in which Carita, as mother and grandmother, was there through this difficult time with her daughter and her three young granddaughters. Granddad Bill was right there very step of the way too, in addition to Carita's mother, her sister and her husband, and other family members, coworkers, and a vast network of friends.

Carita and Bill live in the Del Webb retirement community in Sun City, Roseville, California. Residents held a parking lot sale and a benefit luncheon to raise funds. "Your generosity is overwhelming, and we cannot thank you enough," she wrote. "There are no words adequate to express how we feel."

October 2000: We have good news to share. Elizabeth's tumor remains stable....These tumors are notorious for recurrence. It's been seven months since her craniotomy. Elizabeth has decided to have chemotherapy and will no doubt be starting it quite soon. There is a very new approved chemo called Temodar...that is less toxic than the regular PCV that is usually used for this kind of tumor. We have again been in touch with doctors at Duke University and Johns Hopkins Medical Center, where this chemo is used....

It's all heavy and confusing information to process. Making these decisions weighs heavily on Elizabeth especially, but her family as well....

Angels are still among us. These loving acts mean so very much....We know you care, and that helps on heavy days. We send our thanks and love.

It was Carita who managed Elizabeth's care with such patience and love, providing that special touch to her family and three daughters.

At times, she was frightened, as she admitted: " 'Friends are angels who lift us to our feet when our wings have trouble remembering how to fly' (author unknown). My wings are heavy right now, and I need you, my friends and loved ones, to help carry us."

Within a short time, a friend responded:

Fear not, for I am with you;
Be not dismayed, for I am your God.
I will strengthen you,
Yes, I will help you,
I will uphold you with My righteous right hand.
(Isaiah 41:10, NKJV)

"These words are a constant source of comfort," Carita told me. "They are taped near my computer screen to be read and reread every day."

As Carita drove her daughter and granddaughters to Reno for daily infusions (including Tributyrate which helps chemo penetrate the brain's barrier), she also provided essential fun for the children. "The girls and I visited a zoo; they swam each afternoon; and we took a trip to Virginia City and rode the old steam train."

When Elizabeth, her daughters, and friends went to Hawaii for a few days, Carita and her daughter Rebecca took care of little Sierra. "She's a happy, active, and darling two-year-old who talks nonstop. Could she be related to me, her 'Grammie'?"

But upon her return from Hawaii, Elizabeth became very ill. One of her antiseizure meds caused her pituitary gland and adrenals to stop functioning. It was a frightening time, and Elizabeth became weak and very thin. "It was like taking steps backward," my friend explained. Chemo was postponed.

October 31: Elizabeth was undecided about the chemo treatment.... She prayed, asking God to send her a clear, loud voice about what to do. The next evening, Dr. Henry Friedman from Duke phoned her...."If you want to survive this tumor, Elizabeth, you must have chemo. Start Temodar right away!" Again, God was with us.

Temodar is taken in pill form for five days in each 28-day cycle and then repeated. It seems that a 12-month period is standard, but much depends on how she tolerates the medication and whether the tumor shrinks. Approximately an hour before she takes the Temodar pills, she takes two antinausea pills. Upon her taking the Temodar, we are praying and reciting the verses from our Sunday evening gatherings. As she swallows the pills, we envision them as God's healing power going directly to her brain and specifically to the tumor to dissolve it.

A dear friend of Elizabeth's wrote this: "Let this medicine, like radiation, be the light of God that shines on me."

Requests were made some months previous for those on the e-mail list to send favorite Bible verses, prayers, poems, and whatever we wanted to pass on to be incorporated into a "prayer quilt." In November 2000 Elizabeth received the finished quilt, adding to the Thanksgiving season. "It's a work of art," Carita wrote. "The messages are so meaningful and beautiful." Carita reported that her daughter was tolerating the chemo with few side effects. "This proud grandma can also say that in spite of all that's happened in their little lives, Hannah and Chelsea are A students. We've had glowing reports from their teachers."

Friends from the Bayside Church, Sacramento, continued to provide meals three times a week. Neighbors whom she called "earth angels" helped to "look out" for Elizabeth and provide transportation for her daughters to and from school every day.

> December 9: Elizabeth is doing very well! She completed her second round of chemo and tolerated it beautifully. We thank God for this new drug and the way her body is receptive to it. With this wonderful Christmas season come opportunities for get-togethers, and we're happy that Elizabeth is well enough to attend some. And this grandma gets to baby-sit those great three granddaughters! Last evening the girls and I decorated Great-grandma's tree and helped her. It was such a nice evening....

At the outset of the New Year, Carita sent an update full of good news. The tumor was stable, no growth, and Elizabeth was tolerating the treatments well. Meanwhile, her church continued providing meals.

Inquiries were now reaching Carita from all across the country and overseas—Long Island, North Dakota, Sweden. Carita's progress report was encouraging, as was the news about her grand-daughters. "Little Sierra will be three tomorrow, and she'll be cele-brating with a Winnie-the-Pooh party. She informs me 'I'm not a baby anymore, Grammie,' if I accidentally refer to her as one! Her vocabulary and skills are amazing to us—one smart little cookie."

By March 2001 the tumor remained stable, chemo contin-ued, and Elizabeth asked to see a neuro-oncologist (someone specializing in the brain as well as chemotherapy). Carita joyfully reported, "Lo and behold, there seems to be such a doctor at the University of California at Davis from Duke University...."

> My daily devotional today is a fitting one to share with you: "Those who speak most deeply to our hearts in times of trouble are invariably those who have suffered. They have much to give." I can't put into words what your giving means to Elizabeth and to all of us who love her. Thank you from the bottom of my heart.

In April the wonderful news came that the tumor was shrink-ing! As they compared MRIs, they all saw that the tumor was, indeed, smaller. "We shed happy tears, as you can imagine. We were given more hope in that appointment than we've [ever] been given before. Dr. Chowgar believes that if there is not regrowth of the tumor in the first year, it's highly unlikely that it will occur.... The doctors concurred 'whatever you're doing, keep on doing it.'"

> July: We have a very active lifestyle here. We try to put fun things into the lives of the granddaughters while

keeping the doctor appointments and doing the "chemo week."... Thus one day we all went to the Sacramento Zoo; another evening found all of us at a River Cats baseball game. We try to find joy in each day. The past two have been fun-filled, with fireworks and concerts and even a parade here in Sun City with Hannah and Chelsea riding on our golf cart—Hannah as Uncle Sam and Chelsea as the Statue of Liberty. We had a great time! We're making happy memories for all of us!

She ended that e-mail with a typical upbeat note: "We love you for sticking with us on this tough journey."

It's a journey they are still on, but in November 2001 came this e-mail: "The news we've all been waiting for has become a reality. The P.E.T. scan shows 'a very low probability of cancer cells remaining,' which means that we'll never know for sure. The word 'cure' is never used, but what we have heard is the 'next best thing' according to her neuro-oncologist. Elizabeth's neuro-surgeon said with a broad smile, 'You have the winning ticket.'"

Elizabeth's winning ticket is her faith and trust in God; she's experienced remarkable answers to prayer; she's returned to caring for herself and her children; and she has the assurance that she's in God's hands.

THE CATASTROPHES WE DON'T EXPECT

No one anticipates a loved one coming down with a catastrophic illness. But when it happens, we have an opportunity to prove the reality of our faith. Carita and Bill provided a wonderful example of that. The medical establishment confirms that intergenerational support when such an event occurs is of utmost importance. My daughter was told by one of the doctors who attended Dustin, "Your family's strong faith, prayers, and presence throughout this ordeal have helped in your son's healing. We always see a difference when there is such support."

One children's research hospital I checked with in Memphis, Tennessee, handling 100 to 125 outpatients daily, and with a 48-bed hospital, said that grandparents are commonly involved—in as many as 90 percent of the cases. Much of society today seems to discourage interdependence among generations, but it only takes a situation such as my friends and my family experienced—where everyone rallies to help hold down the family fort, being supportive of each other and available for whatever arises—to realize how dependent we truly are on each other.

THE CONSOLATION OF HOPE

At such times, the nitty-gritty of the illness is very difficult. My daughter, my friend Carita, and I were in agreement: What do people do without strong faith and a firm trust in God? Carita and I, as grandmothers, had been through a lot of life experiences, including losses, and we knew how to glean hope. My daughter was no stranger to heartbreak either, so it was this hope that we were able to hold out to each other and to our loved ones.

Hope is the anchor for the soul. The writer of Hebrews points to the strong consolation available for those "who have fled to take hold of the hope offered to us... We have this hope as an anchor for the soul, firm and secure" (Hebrews 6:18b-19a).

The Bible is full of references to hope, but Psalm 71, in particular, resounds with the cries of an older writer, and I found much comfort in its message that I could pass on.

You are my hope (verse 5). You are my strong refuge (verse 7). I will hope continually (verse 14).

LOVE HELPS CARRY BURDENS

Someone has said that blessed is the child who can run to his grandparents' arms when growing up is difficult. And doubly blessed is the child who knows his grandparents are there for him when he is going through a catastrophic illness.

When we help to bear someone else's burdens, we carry some of it away from them. How true this is when a family member is in a crisis situation brought on by illness! Love is a burden carrier. Love drives us to do things for others that they cannot do for themselves.

Alvin Toffler wrote that the family has been called the giant shock absorber of society, the place to which the bruised and battered individual turns after doing battle with the world, the one stable point in an increasingly flux-filled environment. This becomes especially meaningful when the unthinkables of life intrude. The role of grandparents who care is never more needed than at such a time.

One woman told me that her grandmother taught her a philosophy to use when facing difficult times. The grandmother had developed the philosophy when she was widowed at age 36 and left with seven children to raise alone. "I never saw anything I couldn't do," the grandmother said in her later years. "I would inch up on it a little at a time." This granddaughter carried that grandmother's saying with her to college when the going was tough, and it has stayed with her through the inevitable trying times that come into everyone's life. "Inching up works," she told me with a smile.

Here are some tips for going through health crises:

• Give the family time to accept the diagnosis and create a treatment routine. Try not to be too sensitive if they decide something different from what you think is best. People handle crises differently. Respect the intelligence and feelings of your adult children. Carita's therapist told her, "It's their path, their life."

• Communicate. Learn all you can about the illness. As Carita and my daughter did, use the Internet. Much of what they were able to learn came from their persistence in tracking down everything they could and then following through. Sharing information and talking openly within the family helps keep the lines of communication open and helps to keep the family strong. Both Carita and Rhonda shared with the doctors what they were learning. The doctors were appreciative and supportive of their research.

• Acknowledge your own feelings and fears. God understands. This is no sign of weakness on your part. Cry out to God. I have always loved Psalm 34:4, 6:

I sought the LORD, and he anwsered me;
he delivered me from all my fears.
This poor man called, and the LORD heard him.

Read the Psalms. You will be encouraged and comforted. Share your findings with your loved ones, especially your grandchild or the one who is struggling with the illness.

• Ask for the prayers and help of your minister or priest. The treatment for cancer is a long process—involve your church and its support groups. Elizabeth's church provided meals three times a week, which was a great help. But beyond the practical kind of help that they can (and should) provide is the spiritual support. Your loved one needs to be on your church's prayer list, as do the patient's loved ones. Both Carita and I were able to enlist the prayer support of friends and many churches throughout the country.

• Reach out to your grandchild's siblings. Sisters and brothers hurt also and may have a lot of fear; they may feel ignored and left out; they are saddened by what is happening to their brother or sister. They need to be comforted, encouraged, and helped also. They more than likely have unmet needs. It is a tall order for grandparents to take on the entire family, but do what you can. Extend yourself with God's help, asking for the strength and wisdom you need to keep on keeping on for your loved ones.

• Encourage the sick grandchild to maintain as normal a routine as possible. If the grandchild is a student, a major illness such as cancer will disrupt his schooling, but if he can handle it, encourage him to keep up by studying at home as he feels up to it. Your encouragement can be a big help. Perhaps you can read to the child or help with some research. Such encouragement will say to the sick child that you are confident there will be recovery and so you want to help him keep up with his studies as much as possible.

• Pray with your grandchild. Share Bible verses and passages. Perhaps you can do a Bible study with him. Share from your life experiences. Nurture his faith. This is a wonderful time for you to be the incarnation of unconditional love.

Where Answers Start ©
Of all life's lessons
one truth stands tall,
you cannot lose hope;
you must not fall.
No matter the picture,
no matter what you see,
God is always there,
He always will be.
He can bring change
when no human hands can,
for He is God
and we are mere man.
So, lift up your eyes
and humble your heart,
prayer is the place
where answers start.

—RHONDA LEE PETRILLO, WRITTEN AT HER SON'S BEDSIDE

16

A GRANDPARENTING POTPOURRI

Look to the LORD and his strength;
seek his face always.
Remember the wonders he has done, his miracles....
Ascribe to the LORD, O families of nations,
ascribe to the LORD glory and strength.
—1 CHRONICLES 16:11-12a, 28

I was all but overwhelmed by the enormity of what I received both from grandparents and grandchildren who responded to my inquiries. Grandparents are heroes and heroines, the means for passing on family history and traditions, positive role models, teachers of lessons otherwise unlearned. And as someone said, best of all, they hardly ever get mad! Children without the benefit of the love and attention of grandparents are being cheated out of a valuable treasure. Grandparents are just so special! And every grandparent worth his or her salt has a repertoire of anecdotes and stories to share, not to mention photos!

So here are some stories I enjoyed—a potpourri of grandparenting—the reminiscings of adult grandchildren, the descendants of some wonderful grandparents.

OUR FAST-PACED WORLD

Older grandparents in particular remember a time when the pace was less frantic and time spent with Grandpa and Grandma was vastly different than it is today. One grandmother explained it like this:

> Our lives are fast-paced and different in almost every way, nothing at all like that of my grandparents, who lived in the country on a farm. We live in a city apartment. There is no "home place" at which the family can gather for Thanksgiving or Christmas. But Jesus is the same, and we try to convey His love in our lives in our own way, just as our grandparents did in their own way.
>
> I used to spend summers with my grandparents on the farm, and it was so memorable for me. So I have special arrangements for each grandchild who is old enough to leave home to spend a couple weeks with us in the summer. We have great fun, doting on that one child, giving him or her all the attention. Of course, we don't have chickens to feed, eggs to hunt for, or an outhouse out back, but we have a pool to swim in and a

zoo to visit. The activities are definitely different, but the laughing, singing, playing games, telling stories, and cuddling up at night are the same.

We try also to make a special time to visit each of our children and their families in their homes, giving them our total attention, even if it's only for two or three days once or twice a year. Each of the five families is unique—fast-paced or laid back, neat as a pin or naturally messy, active doers or passive watchers, healthy eaters or junk food lovers, elegant dressers or casual slouchers, Bach lovers or Willy Nelson idolizers, philosophical deliberators or armchair football coaches, outdoor lovers or indoor lovers. Whatever their lifestyle, we try to blend in, doing whatever is pleasing to them.

"Praise the Lord! They all go to church, hold to high moral standards, and basically adhere to our traditional family values, give or take a little here and there. Their deviations from our traditions are nothing so unacceptable to us that we are uncomfortable, nor do we feel the need to confront them. Usually, they will ask us about or discuss a situation with us anyway, which is wonderful.

Our kids had their share of troubles growing up, and some are still suffering the consequences of wrong decisions in the past, but they are learning, changing, and growing in wisdom, which I believe is the whole key—to be willing to learn and change. One daughter told me, "The reason I love you and Daddy with a pure heart is because I could forgive you the things I thought you did wrong when you were raising us kids. The reason I could forgive you so easily is because I saw that you were always trying to learn how to do better, and you were always applying those things to your life to make positive changes. So that's the style of parenting that you see us give our kids now. You modeled it for us."

NATIONAL (FAMILY) HOLIDAYS

Phyllis Seminoff felt it was important for her children and grandchildren to remember the importance of honoring veterans. So one Memorial Day, after good food, conversation, and play, she gathered the little ones and some visiting neighborhood children in her garage and said, "Let's put together a Memorial Day parade." She had carefully thought this through and was prepared to make it a memorable event for her grandchildren.

With red, white, and blue streamers, and one child carrying the American flag high in the air, we marched in parade mode out the side garage door, out the front gate, down the sidewalk in view of all the neighbors, and finally to our front door, where we surprised Grandpa (my husband) and the grandchildren's parents by marching in, singing a patriotic song. The kids never forgot it. One of our sons remarked, "We'll have to do this every year."

What a great idea! With the passing of our generation—those of us who lived through World War II—will go the firsthand memories of those years. It is very important to help our children and grandchildren remember the importance of these special holidays and the sacrifices for the freedoms we hold dear. We have a perspective that needs to be handed on to our loved ones. The courage and heroism of those who fought so valiantly to make and keep America free from dictatorships and tyranny must not be forgotten.

Another grandmother related that Christmas and Easter are times when her family celebrates cherished traditions. "With five children and with grandchildren scattered across the country, we alternate where we spend holidays. But whomever we're with, we observe both Christmas and Easter because of their meaning to the life of Christ. These holidays are times for loving together-ness, which is hard to accomplish in today's complex society, but we work at it."

My own children especially recall Christmas Eve candlelight church services as a family. We could take up a couple of pews. We always had a large gathering for a buffet dinner and exchang-ing of gifts that included two unmarried aunts, an unmarried cousin and her friend, as well as the grandparents, with the chil-dren reenacting the familiar Christmas story from the gospels. The old movies of those events bring tearful memories.

Martha Ashworth tells of the tradition she established for her younger grandchildren.

It was a hands-on way for the children to participate in telling the Luke 2 Christmas story. As I read it from the Bible, they reenacted the event using an unbreakable

Nativity set, which they could easily manage. Everyone participated, even the two-year-old. Each year the grandchildren would add to the verses they had learned and play a different role in the story.

As the grandchildren got older, Martha inaugurated a new tradition.

The grandchildren could invite their friends over for a "Reason for the Season" party. I set up different stations around the house. At the first stop, we had goldfish. We tried to teach them to perform tricks, but the children soon realized you could only communicate with the fish if you became a fish yourself. The message was that God loved the world so much that He became a baby who became a man so we could understand.

The second station was a simple craft they made, and we buried it in a time capsule. The third station was everyone sitting down to hear the Christmas story and a variation of the hands-on Nativity that the grandchildren knew so well. The fourth station was the kitchen, where we made Nativity cookies and hot chocolate and talked about what Christmas really means. Finally, I had a tree and gifts under it for each child to remind them that Jesus was the greatest gift of all.

The children enjoyed this so much that we did it for several years. It then expanded into a community and church outreach at the children's church. There were so many children that we had to take them in groups starting about every 15 minutes. Church mothers and grandmothers helped, and I am sure it will continue for years to come.

Barbara Johnson related that for birthdays and Christmas, instead of giving toys, she and "Gopher Bill" took each of their grandchildren to the local Christian bookstore and let them browse through it with their mother and select what they would like—lacy covers for their Bibles, plaques for the walls in their rooms, little crosses that glow in the dark as prayer reminders. She spoke of the wonderful Christian books and videos and tapes available and how she taught her daughter-in-law the importance of putting on Christian music early in the morning so the children would wake up to the sounds of gospel music, "which is so encouraging. Bill and I have given them such videos and tapes and encouraged them to love Christian music and learn about the artists."

Barb is big on celebrating the first of each month. "My married son and his wife make it a special time—something fun to do for themselves and the children. So does my other son. It makes each new month a fresh start, a new beginning, a whole new month with no messes yet on it."

"HAPPY BIRTHDAY, JESUS"

A Minnesota grandmother wrote of her seven grandchildren and the special sharing time they have at Christmas.

Grandpa reads the Christmas scripture, then we sing Christmas carols. We light candles, each candle representing a grandchild and a large candle in the center for Jesus. We have a birthday cake and sing "Happy birthday, dear Jesus," and then we sing "Come into My Heart, Lord Jesus."...

We are a family who pray together and laugh and cry together. We also celebrate birthdays, providing a time for the cousins to get together and have fun. But it does take some effort to get hold of everyone and find a time when we can all make it.

Phyllis Seminoff relates that for as long as she can remember Christmas Eve has been their family's special time of togetherness.

My most memorable Christmas Eve was Christmas 1999. In retrospect, I know God put it together. Our celebration began in the early afternoon when daughter Dayna called and asked if she could come early and bake cookies. A resounding "yes" to that! Greeting family and friends with the delectable smell of cookies in the oven was a wonderful way to begin our family Christmas gathering.

Knowing that kids, grandkids, and friends had spread throughout the house, an hour or so before dinner I took a walk through, room by room, desiring to observe all the family happenings. In the kitchen I found son-in-law Chip peeling potatoes for dinner while animatedly sharing about his computer business with a friend, Betty. As I walked by the step-down living room, my darling husband, Bill (who was destined to be with the Lord the following Christmas), was sitting on the sofa, before the fire, chatting with our good friend Joe. From their glowing countenances, I could see the joy they were having in one another's company. I went on to the den and found daughter Dayna, her husband, Doug, and daughters Leslie and Mary Jo discussing a little one coming to the family. I walked down the hall to the bedroom area and found son Bruce with his son, Aaron, watching a Christmas video in the children's room. Then, lastly, I put my ear to the master bedroom door and listened to the sounds of granddaughters Emily, Jennifer, and Stephanie practicing a skit they planned to do for entertainment later in the evening, as they waited for other cousins to arrive. In my heart I said, *It's a Norman Rockwell Christmas at its best,* and to this day I cherish the memory of every remembered scene.

FAMILY TOGETHERNESS

Yes, family togetherness does take time and effort in the chaotic, busy world in which we function today. Grandparents are very conscious of the need, however, to maintain family togetherness as much as possible. Family members have to want to maintain togetherness and put forth the effort. When Grandma and Grandpa are gone, in far too many families, aunts and uncles and cousins move all over the country, and once-strong family ties become lost.

Then there are Mother's Day, Father's Day, and Grandparents' Day get-togethers to honor parents and grandparents, with the children bearing gifts they've made or picked out very carefully. What joy!

Weddings of grandchildren—with Grandmother and Grandfather being escorted down the aisle—are such wonderful occasions. On the occasion of my granddaughter Heidi's wedding in Canada, my four-year-old great-grandson was my escort. Oh yes, this was very special! My grandson watched proudly, as did my daughter Tonia. Grandpa was celebrating in heaven, we agreed.

Wanda Sharpe shared the beautiful story of her mother's thoughtfulness. Knowing that she wouldn't live long enough to attend her grandson's wedding, she embroidered pillowcases and crocheted edgings on them. She wrote a letter to this grandson, only 10 at the time of her death, and Wanda was asked to save it until her son's wedding day. "Dear Lee: I know I won't be around when you get married, but I want you and the girl you choose to know how much I loved you. I pray that the two of you will be Christians all your lives. Love, Mimi." Wanda presented it to her son and his bride at the wedding, along with a picture of her mother, Lee's Grandma Mimi. There is a photo of Lee reading the letter that depicts a very emotional moment for the grandson who dearly loved his grandmother. Today that cherished gift is in a beautiful frame, preserved for Lee and his wife to hand down someday to their son and his "girl," as

Grandma Mimi put it. I saw this gift and was deeply moved by what it represented.

FOOD AND FAMILIES

Many grandchildren connect favorite foods with family relationships. "Homemade fresh peach ice cream and angel food cake," a grandson recalled.

Several grandmothers found letting grandchildren help prepare meals was "an opportune time" to teach homemaking skills, in particular, for little granddaughters. "When we have family get-togethers, I involve the grandchildren in a lot of the preparation. Little girls love to help set the table, put the place cards around, the napkins in napkin rings, and decorate with a centerpiece."

My writer friend Vicki Bohe-Thackwell shared a memorable experience that happened in the fall of 2001 and that brought back memories of her grandmother:[1]

I was looking forward to our trip to the mountains of Tennessee. My husband and I had been invited to attend a storytelling festival in the town of Jonesborough. The autumn leaves were bold with color. The historic town, with its cobblestone streets, steepled churches, and friendly people, was a welcome relief after the events of September 11. I had never been to the mountains of Tennessee, but my great-grandmother and great-grandfather came from there. I knew a few stories about them, but I didn't realize, until visiting Tennessee, the ways that those grandparents affected my life.

It started with the chocolate pie. My grandmother made the best homemade chocolate pie. I have lived in so many states, but I have never tasted a pie that tasted like my grandmother's. Then on the third day of the festival, after listening to a talented Christian storyteller, we decided to find a small Southern restaurant to eat in. We found the perfect place. We walked in to see people talking across tables and throwing greetings across the room—locals who had known each other all their lives, from the sound of it. After a lunch of fried chicken, I decided to go all out and have a piece of chocolate pie. I was shocked. The pie tasted just like my grandmother's pie. Then it came to me that my grandmother must have used her mother's recipe—a recipe from Tennessee. You have to understand that I was raised in a military family and never had a sense of hometown or close connections to relatives. Tasting that chocolate pie connected me to my roots in a rush of emotions. Everybody was so friendly in this town that I just started telling the first worker I saw my story of my grandmother and her pie.

To my surprise and delight, this person told me his mother made the pies from scratch every morning at home and he brought them in to the restaurant. I told him to tell his mother how wonderful the chocolate pie was. I said that the only thing missing was the meringue. Do you know that the next morning, just as we were pulling out, a pie was delivered to me? It was still warm from the oven. It was chocolate. It was covered with mounds of golden meringue. It spoke my language.

I've never met the woman who made this for me. We headed home. After an hour, I couldn't stand the thought of that pie cooling down too much. We had only one plastic fork in the car. We stopped on the side of the road in the middle of the beautiful Appalachian mountains, found a patch of grass, and we three—my husband, his niece, and I—ate most of that pie. It was the best pie I ever ate. It was made by a woman who never met me but who understood my yearning to be connected to my grandparents and to my past. I felt so loved. What a contrast to the horrors of September 11 and the attack on America. I realized in that trip that my grandmother's love of stories, her Christian beliefs, and her talent for cooking wonderful pies were part of her inherited culture and that she had passed that down to me, though I saw her only a handful of times during my growing-up years. Generational nurturing is a powerful thing. God was certainly wise when He gave us grandparents. I thank Him for mine.

Another grandmother wrote about "going to the garden to pick greens with Grandpa, and Grandma cooking those fresh veggies. She and I would also go out and pick wildflowers for dinner centerpieces. Grandfather owned a small neighborhood grocery store. I got to pick out my favorite cookies as a treat with milk. Before going to the Saturday night picture show,

Grandfather would let me choose my favorite candy bar to take with me."

This same grandmother told a darling story of her three-year-old grandson.

I sat on the front porch watching him play. He was running his tricycle off the sidewalk and into my flower bed, which had some plants known as "chicken and hens." I called to him, "J. D., don't get in Gran's flowers." He gave me his sweet, innocent little grin, and once again I said, "J. D., those are Gran's chicken-and-hen flowers." I went into the house to start dinner, keeping an eye on him from the kitchen window. Soon he came in and said, "Grandma, I won't get in your fingers and hands flower bed anymore," and he wrapped his little arm around my leg lovingly.

[Another grandson] and I would take walks in the evening. He was probably four years old when he saw a yellow flower called "buttercup." He stooped to pick it for me when I said, "Let's dig it up and plant it." He found a stick with a sharp point, and we dug up the pretty plant. Today, that small plant covers the foundation around our home....

You can be sure that grandparents such as this have nurtured the foundation for understanding and responding to the work of God in their grandchildren's lives. Grandma Phyllis says,

I've thought of the interaction with the grandchildren that we've had through the years—those grandchildren (at this writing) ranging from age 29 to 14 months. I've thought how we worked with them in the daily things of life so they could see how Grandpa and Grandma lived life as Christians. This was "building family," creating a memory book in their minds, just as a memory book had been built into my mind by my grandmother. Grandchildren need to know the scope of their grandparents' love of the Lord.

Another thing I've done is to keep a "Molly box," an "Aaron box," etc., for each of the grandchildren. In each box is every letter, note, card, drawing they ever gave us. This shows my respect for all that they have taken the time to give or send. Then I've included my own special writings for them, words that will prayerfully reinforce our love of the Lord, and the love and care we had for each of them individually, long after we've gone to be with the Lord. Passing on a heritage, giving them memories.

STRONG AND RESOURCEFUL ANCESTORS

Donna Cowsert Morton reminded me that there is much for present and future generations to know about their heritage of strong and resourceful ancestors. She's making certain her grandchildren know the story of their great-grandparents.

Mark and Minta Cowsert left Junction, Texas, in May 1909 by covered wagon headed for Dimmitt (Castro County) in the Texas panhandle. My grandmother, Minta, told me she made my father, Ray Cowsert, his third birthday cake over an open campfire on May 28, 1909. On this trip they had to climb the cap rock to get to the flatlands of the prairie. She said the land was beautiful, with grass as high as their horses. There were small creeks and lakes, with deer, antelope, and buffalo to be seen all along the way. They had maps that followed the buffalo trails. Three other family wagons and two supply wagons were in their wagon train. It was over 400 miles to their destination.

My father and all seven of his siblings attended a two-story red-brick school building that housed all 11 grades. School was across the street from the Cowserts' large brick home, built in 1917. I was born in Dimmitt in 1933 and attended the same school as my father. After school, I would go across the street to Grandmother's for milk and cookies. Grandma Minta was small and trim—only five feet one, with big blue eyes. She was strong and stayed busy with her large garden full of fruit trees, vegetables, and flowers. It was midafternoon when I would find her fresh from a bath, with a pretty dress and her hair freshly coiffed. I asked her why she always dressed like that in the afternoon instead of the mornings. She said she wanted to look her best for my grandfather when he came home from the office.

Grandfather Mark was the county surveyor, abstractor, and attorney. Dimmitt was the county seat. He drove a motorcycle to survey the land. Later he purchased one of the first Model A Fords in the town. He was a dashing man of five feet eleven. He had a mustache that he kept in various fashion. He would let me climb on the back of his armchair in the parlor so I could fix his hair in curls using bobby pins.

Once Grandpa Mark and Grandma Minta took me on a camping trip to New Mexico. I was around six or seven. I remember seeing buffalo in small herds and Indians in their native dress.

One morning Grandma woke me to tell me to come out and see what "Jack Frost" had done during the night. All the leaves were bright red and yellow. It was just beautiful!

On December 7, 1941, a sunny afternoon in Dimmitt, my father (Ray), Grandfather, and I were on their front porch listening to the radio when it was announced that Pearl Harbor had been bombed by Japanese fighter planes. Grandfather thought we would have "the Japanese licked in six weeks." By December 1942, the war was still on. My father enlisted in the Army Signal Corps and served in New Guinea until late 1945, after the atomic bomb was dropped and the Japanese surrendered. My father was 39 when he returned to Hereford to start his law practice anew.

My life changed that December 7, as it did for

millions of people around the world. The small towns of Dimmitt and Hereford changed as almost all eligible men were required to go to war. Located between the two towns, a prisoner-of-war camp was built that held over seven thousand Italian prisoners—more than the population of both towns.

My grandparents were married March 9, 1897. In March 1947 they celebrated their 50th wedding anniversary. They bore eight children—six lived long lives, and they bore 11 grandchildren. Mark Cowsert died in 1949, and Minta preceded him in 1948.

I found Donna's story interesting in that I, too, was listening to the radio on December 7, 1941, in a little Iowa country home. Often on Sunday, following church, friends would invite my mother and me to drive with them some 20 miles to the town where we lived to spend the afternoon visiting relatives. These friends dropped us off at the home of Mother's sister and they went on their way to visit their family. My aunt and uncle were at church—we knew they would be—but the house was unlocked. We went in and Mother turned the radio on to listen to her favorite Sunday afternoon program, *The Old Fashioned Revival Hour*. The program was interrupted with the announcement that the Japanese had bombed Pearl Harbor. Mother's hand flew to her face, she uttered an "Oh no!" and I saw the shock and horror registered there.

Shortly thereafter the relatives arrived home. Everyone greeted the news with the same degree of shock. Memories of

World War I were still with these people. They had a brother-in-law who had been gassed and whose health was in decline. The local cemetery had graves of the war dead who were honored every Memorial Day. Now their sons would be going off to another war. This was grim news. Who would be drafted? Could the farm boys be deferred in order to help grow and harvest crops? It was a sad but memorable day. Some of us would live to tell about it to our grandchildren and great-grandchildren; others would not. Soon the red, white, and blue squares of cloth with stars in the center would appear in the windows of homes across the land—evidence that a son was in the service. When the flags came down and the blue stars were replaced with gold stars, we knew a loved one had been killed.

Years later I was to learn that my future husband, Herman R. Hosier, was singing in the Old Fashioned Revival Hour chorus and in the quartet that Sunday afternoon.

Survivors of World War II are disappearing at the rate of more than a thousand a day. If you are a grandparent and haven't recorded your memories of those days, I urge you to do so. Perhaps you have a grandson or granddaughter who would help you. I know they and your future progeny, some yet unborn, would someday truly value what you could share now. Where were you and what did you do during the war? If you saw action, how did God preserve your life? What did He do for you? Did your war experiences draw you closer to Him? Where did you serve? What was it like?

I sat with Lt. Colonel Earl Mooney in Fullerton, California, a dear friend and loving grandfather, and was able to get him to talk about some of his experiences. He participated in 10 major battles from Casa Blanca in Morocco, all the way along the coastline of the Mediterranean, through France, parts of Germany, to Salzburg in Austria. These were fighting foot soldiers. Fighting included the Anzio beachhead battle in Italy. Fighting in North Africa was intense, and by the time these battle-weary men and women reached Anzio, they were asking, "How much longer can this go on?" But Earl was a survivor.

"How did you survive, Earl?" I asked him.

"It was the Lord and my faith," he responded. "Isaiah 26:3, 'Thou wilt keep him in perfect peace, whose mind is stayed on thee, because he trusts in thee.'"

He was a young man, but his faith was strong. He married, became a father to three sons, and grandfather to six. He is proud to tell you that his oldest grandchild is 28 and the youngest is four. And he would say, with rightful grandfatherly pride and joy, that his oldest grandson has worked in Christian television in Taiwan.

"YOU ALWAYS WIN A BETTER RESPONSE WITH LOVE"

I am thankful for a memory my children share. Rhonda relates it:

> Whenever we would fight or argue as siblings, you would say, "Children, you always win a better response with love." You put a little motto above the light switch in Tonia's and my bedroom and it said: "Keep Sweet."

We couldn't miss it as we went in and out of our room! We saw it often enough and I think it helped us to remember and try.

You used Scripture verses over and over, Mom, and you would say, "Love one another" or "Be ye kind," or "Love the Lord your God with *all* your heart, and with *all* your mind." Just short reminders, but I can hear you say, "Serve others; don't return evil for evil; do what's right," and "Trust and obey." You didn't say, "Don't do that!" or words to that effect. Scriptures were convicting and the authority came from not just Mom but from God. We responded to that. You weren't pushy or preachy; it was just your way. I also remember your saying to Dad, "Don't let the sun go down on your wrath," when he would be upset about something and wouldn't communicate. I learned from all of this, and it's what I've sought to do with my family.

Yes, I've seen how my grandchildren have learned from and responded to this just as their mother did.

Special Outings with Grandparents

The children remember the special outings with grandparents. Rhonda writes: "I remember camping in the trailer at O'Neil Park. I remember eating breakfast at the little table by the window and watching the squirrels—the Bible was on the table between the salt and pepper. Funny I should remember that so distinctly," my daughter says. "And Gram always read the Bible at mealtimes. She loved God's Word."

They remember, too, the occasions when this grandma took each of them out for a fast-food lunch. "It was such a big deal," they recall. "Grandma took such delight in doing it. And then we'd have one of our good talks. It was just the two of us. So special."

TRANSITION TIME

The Guffees, a Texas couple, told of the divorce of their daughter, who was left without means to support herself and her son.

Because of the situation with my daughter and our grandson, we built a new home with them in mind, and now we all live together. It was a terribly difficult transition time for our grandson—he was very confused and sad—but the security he has received from us as loving and steady grandparents, and from a mother who loves him dearly, is making a wonderful difference. We are able to give him a good Christian school education, and his caring teachers have also made a huge difference in his behavior. We are all members of the same church and very active there.

His grandfather, my husband, is setting a good example of a godly man who builds up and doesn't tear down, who will never leave us, and who keeps his promises. My husband is really into his computer, and so he and our grandson find much to enjoy, do, and talk about together.

A SHARED HOSPITAL ROOM

In a get-acquainted time at a church function, Evelyn Hinds met Tom Jones, 42, who shared the story of his life with her.[2] "An unexpected and extended time with my elderly grandfather changed my life," Tom said.

Tom was born with heart abnormalities that would usually cause death by age 12. However, God had other plans for him. Looking at his ample, six-foot frame today, it's hard to imagine that at age 18 he stood five feet one and weighed 90 pounds. It was then that his family journeyed from their native Texas to Birmingham, Alabama, to a hospital where Tom was to have major heart surgery.

While Tom was in the hospital, his near-90-year-old grandfather came from Crockett, Texas, to visit him. "Pa Pa's heart stopped while he was in the hospital waiting room. Because he was so near medical help, a rush of hospital personnel came to revive him. His heart was brought back to life, and Pa Pa was given a pacemaker."

The hospital conveniently assigned Pa Pa the other bed in young Tom's room. It was there that they spent 24 hours a day together for the next six weeks while they convalesced. It was during those shared moments that Tom was privileged to get to know his grandfather in a way that most of Pa Pa's other 30-some grandchildren hadn't.

Tom recounted that his grandfather shared many of his impressions of history that he had lived through—the first time he saw a car, the first World Series, the first world war, and many other milestones of his long life. But most of all, woven through these stories, Pa Pa shared his faith. Tom explained that while Pa Pa was active in his church, he never held to a form of religion. Tom brightened as he remembered, "Pa Pa lived in a state of grace." Undoubtedly those lessons of a faithful life fell on ears that were prepared to hear.

Within six months of being released from the hospital, Tom grew to be six feet tall and weighed 170 pounds. Grandfather lived five more years. The time together had changed Tom in more significant ways inside than even his heart surgery. Today he carries his grandfather's legacy of grace to any who will listen.

IN THE SWEET BY-AND-BY

Karolyn Guentherman wrote about the precious memories of her grandmother singing hymns and gospel songs while she went about her many chores as a farmer's wife. "A vivid memory is of grandmother singing 'In the Sweet By-and-By' as she poured fresh cow's milk into the separator located in a little shed beside their modest farm home."

> My grandparents attended the Baptist church in a small, central Kansas town. I especially liked to visit when they were having tent revival meetings. The book table on the right side of the pulpit was always very interesting to me. This was my introduction to the Grace Livingston Hill books. Grandmother always bought me at least one new book. Those books were a strong contributor to my value system and dating relationships.

Today, Karolyn is an exemplary grandmother who gives unstintingly of herself to her grandchildren, and her love of music and books is very evident in her home and lifestyle. She is passing on that appreciation and love to her grandchildren. Moreover, her faith is unwaveringly strong even though in 2000 her husband, the children's grandfather, died. She has taught and assured them that Grandpa is with Jesus. They adore their grandma.

GRANDMA GARDENER

An amazing 87-year-old grandmother, Grandma Gardener, told about her great-grandfather.

> He was one of the truest Christians I have ever known. After the death of his wife, he often visited us, some-times staying two or three months. Each day he would have me read from his Bible to him. He loved the Word of God. I do still wonder sometimes if he selected passages for my good or his! Probably both.

Imagine, in her late 80s, still wondering about her great-grandpa! (I loved that sense of humor I detected there!)

This woman's son, Taylor, received the family legacy of faith, accepted it, nurtured it, and became a minister of the gospel working alongside Dr. Charles Swindoll. His mother's great-grandfather would have praised God. Here is a third-generation progenitor carrying on what was begun in the heart of a believing great-great-great-grandparent.

Grandmother Gardener mentioned discussing the social issues of the day with her grandchildren. "Abortion, homosexuality, divorce, whatever is going on—oh yes, I stay informed." Amazing! She's probably better informed, especially from a Christian perspective, than some people in their 20s and 30s.

"GRANDFATHER RANG THE BELL"

Another grandmother, whose name is Martha, wrote a darling story about her grandfather, who was responsible for ringing the church bell each Sunday morning in their small community.

> He would take me along and let me hold on to one end of the rope. As he pulled on the other end, I would go up in the air, ringing the bell. We would sing, "Ring Those Bells." And he would say, "We're inviting people to come worship God," and remind me that I was doing my part. That made me feel happy and needed. That is one of my first memories of church, love of God and Jesus, and our family worshiping together in church. The church was a big part of our whole family life. What a great foundation our grandparents started for us!

GRANDMA'S GIFT OF LISTENING

This same Martha spoke lovingly about her grandmother:

> One of the biggest gifts she gave me was that she always took the time to listen. She taught me a lot about life

that I have used all through the years. One incident that was very important to me comes to light. I reached my height of five feet seven by the time I was twelve. I was also very thin. Being a girl, that wasn't good. I was constantly teased at school and called "Bird legs." I came home crying many times. My grandmother consoled me, teaching me to accept myself and to learn to laugh at myself. She told me that Jesus made me the way I was. He loved me as I was. He was in my heart and always with me. Those who were calling me names and teasing me were missing a lot if they didn't get to know me regardless of my outward appearance. She taught me that we are all dearly loved children of God.

What I learned from my grandmother I have sought to pass on to my own grandchildren—by being there, whether just to listen, to encourage them, to cry with them, or to praise them.

How important for us as grandparents to have listening ears, but even more importantly, hearing hearts!

A GRANDMA'S SACRIFICIAL CHRISTMAS GIFT

One of the most cherished memories of my 19 years as a Christian bookseller relates to the work-wizened, dear little elderly lady, stoop-shouldered and walking with a limp, who came into our bookstore. Opening up her well-worn purse, she found a coin purse and, turning it upside down on the counter, said,

"This is what I have to spend, and I want a Bible for my grandson." She paused, wiped a tear from her eyes, and added, "He's in the service."

"Tell me about your grandson," I urged. With pride in her voice, she related how he'd enlisted in the navy and how this would be his first Christmas away from home.

"I miss him so much," she added, taking a hanky out of her purse and using it to wipe away more tears. "He was always so good to me and made Christmas special."

I had selected several Bibles that I felt would be right for a young navy man. "Oh, those are too expensive," she said, handling them with care.

"I don't think so," I responded. "You've saved quite a bit here."

"Ohhhh, have I really? You see, I do night janitor work over at the mall."

You can be sure her pennies, nickles, dimes, and quarters were blessed and multiplied by the Lord. "He is going to love this one," she brightened. "Navy blue, too—just right for a sailor. I led him to the Lord when he was just a little guy."

My prayers for her and her dearly loved seaman grandson followed her out the door and for a long time afterward. How many of these sacrificial gifts from grandparents have found their way to grandchildren? I can't help but wonder how God has blessed both the givers and the receivers.

17

THE JOY OF GRANDPARENTING

A good name is more desirable than great riches;
to be esteemed is better than silver or gold.
—Proverbs 22:1

It was with much anticipation that I accepted an invitation to stay at the home of Larry and Marlene Lee in Saint Paul, Minnesota. Almost immediately upon meeting this dear couple, I sensed that I was going to enjoy myself. There was an instant rapport. We had so much common ground—much to share with each other about our love for the Lord, the things He has taught us, the things we were still learning, the experiences of our lifetimes in raising our families, and now the joy of grandparenting.

"Oh, you must come see the grandchildren's playroom," Marlene said, and down we went to the lower level of the house. I could have stayed there for the rest of the trip. Hats and dress-up clothes, grown-up's shoes to clomp around in, ladies' purses, gloves, jewelry, scarves. Oh, to be a child again—oh, to be one of Marlene's grandchildren!

Then I spotted the books. What a great assortment! Shelves of them. "May I peek?" I asked, and I pulled a well-worn volume off the shelf.

"One of my daughter's favorites when she was little," Marlene explained. "Kind of worn." *Worn*—my imagination took wings. I saw that cute little girl sitting alongside her beautiful young mother. "Let's read *this one,* Mommy," and off it would come from the shelf.

Both Marlene's daughter, Michelle, and her son, Nathan, became book lovers. "Nathan took off with books like jet lightning," Marlene said. "To this day he has an incredible reading and retention ability. He loves to read!"

The old saying came to mind: "Books are keys to wisdom's treasure." Now I was anxious to meet those children who had benefited so much by their mother's love of books, which she had passed on to them. I knew I was in for a real treat when I met Marlene's grandchildren. "My children were crazy about books," she said, "and now my grandchildren love to be read to and are going to learn to read on their own. I saved all my children's books for this very day," she added with a wistful expression on her face. "It gives me pleasure to see them handle these books with such care."

But it wasn't just books. I glanced around the grandchildren's playroom. There were boxes of games, some with familiar names recalling my own children's love for box games when they were younger. And toys. Fun things to delight the heart of any child. Dolls, cars—little boy and girl playthings.

Still there was more. Songbooks, cassette tapes, videos. "I'll bet you baby-sit a lot," I laughingly said. I was recalling her invitational letter, in which she had stated, "Very often my five grandchildren are here (all under the age of five)."

"And we love every minute of it," she responded with a big smile. "In fact, we'll be baby-sitting my son's children tomorrow night. We're going out for dinner tonight and you'll get to meet everyone."

Marlene and Larry were some of the neatest grandparents I've ever encountered. Having her son's little daughter, Elizabeth, still a toddler, and three-year-old grandson, Nicholas, around the next night was an eye-opening experience as I saw Grandmother Marlene in action. Here was Lois personified. Sitting at the kitchen table, Marlene read a Bible story to the two little ones while they ate their food. In between reading, she would check to make sure they weren't creating a mess by playing with the food. They were well-behaved children, and besides, they were too interested in Grandma's story to make a mess or fuss. The story of David, the shepherd boy, was one of their favorites, and it's what Nicholas asked for.

Afterward, Nicholas politely asked if he could go and play in the playroom. Soon he came bounding up the stairs dressed in a cowboy outfit. He had to show off to "Papa" Larry and "Nona" Marlene and the strange lady visiting his grandparents.

A Passion for Music

Marlene's and her daughter Michelle's passion is music. They team teach a program for which they are early childhood music educators. Partnering with the Northwestern College Academy of Music in the early childhood music program, "KinderStudio of Musik" is music- and movement-based learning at its finest to nurture the total development of children. The program is based on research showing that consistent musical exposure during the "sensitive and critical" period of a child's life greatly improves children's musical enjoyment, understanding, and achievement. Martin Luther would have appreciated what was taking place.

> I wish to see all arts, principally music, in the service of Him who gave and created them. Music is a fair and glorious gift of God. I would not for the world forego my humble share of music.... Music makes people kinder, gentler, more staid and reasonable. I am strongly persuaded that after theology there is no art that can be placed on a level with music; for besides theology, music is the only art capable of affording peace and joy of the heart.... The devil flees before the sound of music almost as much as before the Word of God.   —Martin Luther

In many of the musical activities, the parent participated with the child. It was an interactive learning experience incorporating children's folk songs, as well as classical music, with the latest research in children's developing systems. The bonding taking place as the adult caregiver and the child moved to the music together was a sight to see. Marlene and Michelle were devoted to their young students, hugging them, listening to the excitement in their voices as they shared things, showing love in demonstrable ways. Mothers, grandparents, and fathers sat on the sidelines when they weren't actively participating in one of the music exercises. It was a happy time for everyone, and it showed as they sang, clapped, moved, and responded to the music, all led by their teacher, Michelle, as Marlene played the piano. Mother and daughter were awesome as they gave of themselves wholeheartedly. *Here is a Grandmother Lois and Mother Eunice,* I thought.

"Sometimes the parents can't afford it, so the grandparents very often step in," Marlene explained. "For some of them, it is a sacrifice—they give up 'things' to invest in their [grand]children." These mothers, too, were Eunices; the grandmothers, Loises. It was a very moving experience for me.

I imagine that if Timothy's mother and grandmother could have done this, they would have.

How good it is when parents and grandparents seize these teachable moments. Marlene exemplified what a godly grandmother can do, and not just for her own grandchildren, but as an extension of herself and the gifts God has entrusted to her for others. Surely this is what the psalmist had in mind when he declared:

From everlasting to everlasting
the LORD's love is with those who fear him,

and his righteousness with their children's children—
with those who keep his covenant
and remember to obey his precepts. (Psalm 103:17-18)

FOSTERING FAITH

Marlene and I talked about the challenges and joys of grandparenting. I asked her, "How do you foster faith in children?"

By believing in them. There is an innate faith already present within the child. God has already placed faith within them. Our job as parents and grandparents is to foster and draw it out.... We want these precious children to know God personally. I did foster and nurture a relationship with my own children, and my husband and I took it upon ourselves to read the Scriptures daily to them at the breakfast table and to pray for and with them before going off to school. We read Bible stories and storybooks with them before bedtime; we prayed blessings before a meal; we took them to church and talked with them about God and Jesus. Our children were also schooled at Christian schools.

I saw my mama (the children's grandmother) and heard her praying beside her bed every morning. I heard her name each of us, her 11 children, and later, after we were all married, I know she added the spouses and then her grandchildren. I was determined to set that kind of example for my children.

In March 1974 I attended Evelyn Christenson's

prayer seminar and I learned a new method of praying. Instead of praying what I wanted to happen and results I wanted—answers, in other words—I began to learn how to pray God's will. So I began to pray requests to God, not answers, and it was a turning point in a deeper walk with the Lord for me. I began a deep, spiritual devotional time each morning, and I started journaling—requesting and recording answers to prayers. The children would come into my bedroom and say, "Mommy, are you through praying yet?" My most important priority became spending time with the Lord and setting an example for them.

Children's literature is very dear to my heart. I studied that subject in graduate school. *Honey for a Child's Heart* by Gladys Hunt was the single most helpful book to me as a young mother. The subtitle of that book is *The Imaginative Use of Books in Family Life.* That appealed to me. The whole book was a wonderful introduction to being a "joyful dispenser of honey to those you love." My children took their love of books with them into their parenting, and now I have the joy of seeing my grandchildren loving books and learning to read.

Hanging on the hallway wall in the Lee home were plaques with the names of everyone in the family and the scriptural meaning of their names alongside.

Marlene gave me the Bible verses that have been the most

instrumental in shaping her life—her marriage, parenting, and now grandparenting. "This is the legacy I want to leave my grandchildren and great-grandchildren," she said.

Later, she wrote and delightedly shared what had happened during family devotions on Sunday, August 5, 2001, during a lengthy discussion about persecuted Christians in China and the recent imprisonment of a Christian missionary.

Our five-year-old grandson, Brock, great-grandson of my mother, son of Michelle, our daughter, was all ears. He is our "Timothy," and he responded by showing us a picture of Baal in his Bible. Then he said, "This is what their god in China looks like [Buddha]." He then volunteered to pray. This was the essence of his prayer: "Dear God, thank You for this day. Fill us with Your joy coming down from heaven. Please help the man who went to jail; help him not to be afraid. Help the bad policemen to know that their god is made of stone and cannot hear them and is not real. Help them to know that You are the real God and You listen and answer when we pray. Help the whole world have peace in You. Amen." He then went around and touched each one of us on the head (we were sitting on the floor) and said, "That was your blessing." He's got it! Our Timothy!

18

EXPERIENCE-BASED WISDOM

I looked for a man among them who would build up the
wall and stand before me in the gap on behalf of the land
so I would not have to destroy it, but I found none.
—EZEKIEL 22:30

Have you ever considered the heritage of faith that was passed on by ancestors? A fairly large number of respondents wrote about such grandparents from the "old country." If they had left their faith behind in the old country, what would have happened in the colonies of this country? When they stepped upon the shores of this land and made their migration west, would they have been able to handle the hardships they encountered without their strong faith? Quite possibly, some among us are going to be the last generation who can look back and reflect on those pioneers from personal experience.

WELSH GRANDPARENTS

Howard and Margaret Smith of Sunnyvale, California, are no longer living, but a letter from Margaret in 1989 carries an important message:

> My grandfather and grandmother were Welsh. They came to America like many others for a better life. They were Methodists from the original church of John Wesley. I have their hymnbook, dated 1823—just words, no notes. They settled in a small town in Colorado and had a general store, which burned down later for lack of water to put out the fire. Times were not easy for them. They expressed their religious beliefs in their actions by helping those in need, giving loans without any paperwork, just a handshake. They were not always paid back.
>
> On Sunday you went to church and spent the rest of the day quietly with family and friends. Church was an important part of their life. You never played cards or did business on Sunday. The many stories of their life came down to our children, and they benefited from them.... The wisdom of these grandparents became my goals in life, and our children were the recipients of what we had learned....
>
> My husband's mother lived with us for 34 years. My daughters benefited from this because she was a fine Christian woman and they loved her very much. It

was necessary to provide a home for her, and our daughters learned to give up having separate bedrooms in a three-bedroom home. They were eight years apart, and this wasn't easy for them, but they learned early that if you love someone, you want to help her. Later, we had four bedrooms and they spent much time in Nanna's room and listened to her advice and Christian teaching.

Howard and I are better grandparents because of our parents and grandparents. My mother's advice to me as a teenager was "You will know right from wrong." She was right; I did. The inner voice spoke to me. The old-timers would call it your conscience. I came to understand it was the Holy Spirit.

A Brave Dutchman

An Iowa man wrote to tell of his great-grandfather who, before he left Holland, attended a state-run church, where the teaching and preaching went against everything he understood from the Bible. At his last service in this church, he got up in the meeting and loudly said, "People, people, do not believe this man. He is telling you nothing but lies, not the Bible truth." This great-grandson has carried that memory with him throughout his life.

A Grandmother from Norway

Fern Lindquist wrote beautifully about her grandmother:

Malena Gjersvig, my precious grandmother on my mother's side, was born in Kahvoda on a mountainside overlooking Masfjord, about 50 miles north of Bergen, Norway.

Her job as a young girl was to tend sheep and milk goats on the pasturelands of the mountain plateau. She made the goat milk into cheese. She would spend the entire summer on the mountain, living in a small building called a "hutter." In the winter she lived with her family and would row across the fjord daily to attend school.

Her future husband, Haaken, worked his way to America as cabin boy on a ship. In America he worked as a farm laborer for seven years, earning $15 a month. Finally he saved enough to return to Norway to claim his bride. On the day following their wedding, Malena and Haaken immigrated to the United States to gain a more secure future for the family they hoped to have. They rented a farm near Emmons, Minnesota, and later were able to purchase an 80-acre farm near Detroit Lakes, Minnesota. How they worked! Pulling stumps, clearing the land. Grandfather then built their home, which still stands today more than a hundred years later, occupied by a great-grandson.

Both grandparents were godly, faithfully attending

the Norwegian Lutheran Church. Their home was always open to traveling pastors. Many times services were held in their home before the church building was constructed. There was no drinking, smoking, or quarreling in their home, which included six children. The oldest was Anna, my own special mother. Grandfather died of cancer in 1920, and Grandmother was left to raise the family alone—alone but for her faith in God and her trust in Him that He would supply their needs. And He did.

Grandmother often came to our home. Her life influenced my own mother, and I'm grateful for such a rich heritage. How we children loved our grandma and her gift of telling stories! Her experiences in Norway made me long to see her native land. It was an emotional experience, therefore, when my dear husband, Rex, took me to Norway and I actually sat in her little white church on the magnificent Solheim fjord. Tears coursed down my cheeks in gratitude for her godly life. She made the Bible come alive as she revealed its wealth, and we children would beg her to "tell one more story."

My own mother and father sacrificed so that I might go to Northwestern Bible College in Minneapolis, but best of all, their example taught me to love and serve the Lord Jesus Christ. What a wonderful day it will be when we can renew fellowship with all of them in heaven!

THE IRISH GRANDFATHER

Bonnie Campbell, whose beautiful story of one of her grand-mothers you've already heard, wrote about her Irish great-grandfather and grandfather.

Pap, as we always called him, lived in the same house all of his life. His father had left Ireland as a young man and settled in Clarion, Pennsylvania. Just a few days after arriving in America, he was asked to guard the body of President Lincoln as it lay in state. Great-grandfather was asked to do this because of his great size—a feature that my grandfather was to inherit.

Pap was a very industrious man, with a keen mind that he retained throughout his life. As a young man, he worked building a railroad tunnel and received several 20-dollar gold pieces for payment. These pieces remain in our family to this day. With his insight, he kept them and gave one to each of his three sons. He was a blacksmith for the local town. He also ran a sawmill and was the president of his own gas company.

He had a great sense of fun and would do almost anything asked of him that was in good taste. Nothing or no one was beneath him. He loved to joke and tease, and when I was a child, it took me a long time to catch on that if you saw his mustache twitch it meant that he was pulling your leg and had probably been doing so for quite some time.

I am still amazed at his mind. He had only a sixth-grade education, but he knew many things that couldn't be taught in a school. He believed that anything was possible if you worked, hoped, prayed, and believed enough. He had such strong faith. In his 80s he decided that he needed another garage, so he set about building it himself. At the age of 96 he suffered a stroke while putting up wallboards in his house. The doctors believed he would die within 24 hours; he lived for 64 more days. He died less than two days before he was to be moved from the hospital to a nursing home. I think he knew that it was his time. He saw a lot in his time. He lived through half of the presidents of the United States, and from horse-drawn carriages to spaceships landing on the moon.

GRANDPARENTS FROM ITALY

Marlene Lee acquired her love of the Bible and her devotion to children from daughter Michelle's grandmother. Michelle Lee Thomson tells the story:

> My grandparents were Catholic when they emigrated from Italy. Grandpa Joe came to the Lord through a hunger in his heart for more of God and His Son, Jesus, and through reading the Bible on his own in this country. His testimony was "short and sweet." He would say, "Whereas once I was blind, now I can see."

Marlene chimes in, relating, "It would be another three months before my mother would even think about going to the little church where he was attending with other Italian relatives and believers. She said that, when she arrived at the door and touched the door handle, she heard the Christians singing 'Victory in Jesus,' and she said to God, 'Please-a-God, if these a-people are-a going to-a-heaven, make-me-a-one!' "

To hear Marlene speak of those dear parents, and to listen as her daughter talks so lovingly about her grandparents, is to join in praising God for the simple faith of those dear ones who parented 11 children. Marlene recalls:

> Just before my father passed away, he said to those of us standing around his bedside, "Whatever church you go to—if they love Jesus—you can worship there with them." Church became so important to him and my mother, and it's important to my husband and me, our two children and their spouses, and our five grandchildren. Then my father said, "Whatever you do, don't forget the name of Jesus." It was precious, so like my dear Italian father. As he breathed his last breaths, he raised his hand heavenward, and I said, "Papa, do you see Jesus?" and he answered, "Yes, He's coming for me," and then he was gone. I have never forgotten it.

Michelle's memories of her grandmother Josephine Runco Testa are, in her words, "all pleasant and satisfying." She recalls,

> We prayed together at her round table in a small Italian kitchen with smells of basil, garlic, and tomatoes. In the

background, her small transistor radio would be tuned to the AM Christian radio station. On the table, before we ate, we would draw a small card from a replica bread loaf—this daily bread was the Word of God, verse by verse. Grandma loved it when I could finally read the verse because she couldn't read or write English. It brought her joy to see me, one of her 36 grandchildren, reading Scripture. Her large black leather Bible had a prominent place in her living room. Almost every visit, she would ask me to read from it for her. In her broken English and strong Italian accent, she would express her appreciation.

She gave a dollar to everyone with whom she came in contact. She remembered all of her grandchildren's birthdays, the TV evangelists, and any new child or visitor who came to her little white house with its yellow trim. Each received a dollar. Grandma received a small Social Security check, less than $400 per month, but was well cared for by the generosity of her children. She gave generously, as though she was the richest lady in town. To me, she was the richest in spirit. She taught me that even one dollar matters!

Everyone—and I really mean *everyone*—loved my grandma. She was the lady with no enemies. That was because she truly lived the way God intended for His people to live. Some of her biblical principles that I heard expressed or saw in action were these: forgive; don't hold grudges; love your enemies; pray for those who despitefully use you; let things go over; love your husband; feed the poor; help the needy and missionaries; go to church every Sunday; volunteer weekly; keep clean; grow your own garden; take time for your family; treat your neighbors right; share whatever you have; pay your bills on time; fix things that are broken; say thank-you all the time; mind your own business; "if you can't say something nice, don-na say it at all"; don't gossip; and get along with your family. Do you think I'm exaggerating? I'm really not. In fact, I couldn't begin to describe the simple yet profound way my grandma expressed her faith by who she was.

One daily occurrence for her was kneeling beside her bed and praying for her entire family by name. That was no small feat—11 children who had 11 spouses who had 36 grandchildren (and now 55 great-grandchildren, plus great-great-grandchildren). Grandma knew everyone's names. I know because I saw and heard her praying for all of them, and I would hear her pray for me. I had the unique privilege of living with my grandma my junior year in high school, as she needed some help and support. We would sit hand in hand on the sofa, my head resting on her unusually soft shoulder. She could sense emotions and had wisdom to guide. She thought I was "fragile" and "a good girl." Her opinion of me mattered and shaped my perception of myself. Grandma believed in me and Grandma believed in God.

My fondest memories and thoughts about my grandma are the frozen orange juice popsicles that she made for us; her yellow wooden teeter-totter; her apple and pear trees with sap dripping down; her vegetable garden; her basement playroom with an old piano, a child-sized table, a tablecloth, a rubber ball, a doll, a stack-up toy, and coloring books; her cellar full of canned food; her homemade, hand-cut raviolis for her family picnic every summer; her pink powder puff in the bathroom that she used.... She was classy—she wore beautiful, colorful dresses with matching gloves, hats, shoes, and purses. She never wore pants—she didn't even own a pair! She had cotton "housedresses" and "going-out dresses." I rarely wore pants to her house, because I disliked her disapproval.

The best part of Grandma was her everlasting hugs, kisses, and feeding us! Her fridge was always full, her stove always hot and cooking something, and her attitude was one of "Eat! Eat more! Eat and be happy!" Her house had a distinct smell, a special aroma of warmth and love.

Michelle carried on these family traditions from her grandmother and her mother in many ways:

We eat together daily, lighting a candle at everyday meals to make them special. Praying together and having a pleasant mealtime conversation where everyone is included. Mom (me), not the children or dad, is responsible for cooking and making delicious, nutritious meals. Wearing an apron when you cook (very Italian!).

We give all year 'round whenever it is in our hand to do. Simple presents to celebrate the everyday. One present per person at Christmas. Quality things, not junk. Give of *yourself*, be kind, thoughtful.

We read and sing lullabies. No bedtime crying at our house. Story reading on the sofa—Dad puts our son to sleep with stories and I rock my two girls to sleep, singing songs to them and God.

We pray at bedtime and mealtime. Photos of missionaries displayed prominently at our home are a reminder to pray for them. We offer our home with a "prophet's chamber" to entertain strangers unaware.

We celebrate big-time birthday bashes with fun themes. My grandmother made angel food cakes—they were her specialty, hung upside down to cool on the green 7-Up glass bottles.

Churchgoing and church life are an integral part of living. Be involved! Know your pastor and his family. Bring your Bible to church. Pay attention. Get to know others.

We go vacationing, with an emphasis on family camp. I grew up going to a week-long revival-type camp, sawdust on the floor and just a lot of singing and preaching. I have now found such a camp for our family. It's a wonderful tradition to carry on and a real vacation for Mom (because I don't have to cook!). The whole week is centered on Christ.

Music! I can't say enough about music! We sing for every occasion. When we're happy or sad, we always have music playing. We also do real live music from the piano, flutes, trumpets, banjo, harmonicas, sticks, shakers, bells.... We sing many prayers at mealtime. There's always a song in my heart. My mother tells how before her mother's death (at age 92), she asked her, "Mama, how come you allowed me to practice the piano when it was time to do dishes (with 11 children there were a lot of dishes and pots and pans)? You would say I had to practice the piano," and my grandmother had replied, "Because I knew someday you would get married and have children and then you would learn how to do dishes, but it would be too late to learn how to play the piano!" My grandmother saved 50 cents from her grocery money so my mother could have piano lessons. She was a very wise grandmother. I owe everything I learned about practicing the piano to my grandmother and my mother.

We create a sense of belonging. It's hard to describe this tradition, but it's very Italian, very family, very fun! It's a part of belonging to a great family of aunts, uncles, and cousins and knowing who they are. Weddings are wonderful. Funerals are farewells. We love the excuse to be together for any event. Annual reunions are just one of many times we get together. Tuesdays in the summer are cousin day! We eat, we talk, we pray together. I could call any of my family any time and they'd be there for me.

We talk. No matter where we are, we talk together. Calling home is important. Daily updates are integral to healthy family relationships.

Michelle asked her talkative son Brock (age five) and daughter Madeline (age four) to tell what they like about their Grandma Nona in some specific ways:

My Nona: "Plays racquet tennis; Plays Candyland game; Plays badminton."

What I like at her house: "Ride my bike on Nona's flat driveway; Playing with her dollhouse."

How she lets us know she loves us: "Thinks we are nice; Tells me I'm pretty; Has a little table for me; Tells us she love us."

Nona prays to God. That's how I know: "She loves God; She does the right things."

"Now I'm done answering questions!"

"Now I'm done answering questions!" Does that sound like any children you know? From the mouth of babes—true, unadulterated wisdom.

STANDING IN THE GAP

When I think about a wise man of God whom God has chosen to use widely, Dr. Charles ("Chuck") R. Swindoll comes to mind. Experience-based wisdom is what you receive from Chuck. This is what he says about his "granddaddy":

> As I was growing up, my most pleasant memories go back to the treasured hours I spent with my "granddaddy" in South Texas. That man knew me and loved me like no one else on earth. Being with him was the fulfillment of my dearest childhood dreams. To this day I recall his wise counsel, his godly perspective on life, his keen sense of humor, his generous spirit, his common-sense approach to problems, and his frequent, warm, affectionate embraces. I respected him as though he never made a mistake. My life was immeasurably enriched by him. The day of his death was one of the most difficult experiences I ever endured. I live in the legacy of his personal investments.[1]

In *Rise and Shine,* Chuck talks about Timothy and his godly grandmother's and mother's training. He also mentions his wife's identification with Timothy. "Cynthia would say, 'It was my mother and my mother's mother who shaped me.' I would say, 'It was my maternal grandfather.' L. O. Lundy of El Campo, Texas, was his name—a man of truth, an example of integrity and godliness."

Chuck tells of a trip he and his daughter Colleen made through Texas in the fall of 1987.

> We decided to take a few blue highways and drive through my home town. I had not returned there for

over thirty years. We drove into El Campo and finally located my grandparents' home. Almost immediately after parking in front of that place where my grandparents lived many years earlier, my tears began to flow. And so did Colleen's. She has heard me speak often of his influence on my life. She read my mind. I looked at an old, stately house where there once lived a great

---

Do you have some models to follow? I am not referring to saints in sculptured stone we place on pedestals and consider perfect. No. The models that sway our lives are very human—and therefore imperfect. Nevertheless, they are great examples to us. They motivate us to live better lives. They may have already lived and died.... The apostle Paul said to Timothy, "You follow my example; if you do, you can make it." ... Models of the faith [are] worth following. Follow them!... The sincere faith that ultimately marked Timothy's life first resided in his grandmother Lois and his mother Eunice. It was Timothy's mother and maternal grandmother who shaped his early spiritual growth. His faith became sincere as he learned of Christ at their knees, sitting under their tutelage.... If your past, like Timothy's, includes a godly heritage, you have been wonderfully blessed. The severity and depravity of these last days will not overwhelm you. You will find strength and stability in the midst of the storm.   —CHARLES SWINDOLL[2]

gentleman. What I remembered most is the love he demonstrated as he took a little grandson on his knee and spoke kindly to him and modeled righteousness and shaped his thinking. Naturally, neither he nor I had any idea where my future would lead me. As she and I sat out front, looking at the windows and the front door and the porch and the little walkway, I was overwhelmed with gratitude. I remembered the truth and I remembered the one from whom I had learned the truth.

Who was it with you? Whom could you name? Were you blessed with parents who loved God? Are you blessed with grandparents like that? ... Don't let the speed of today cause you to treat the depth of your past lightly. Return to the truth of your past. Review those lives and those events. Remember them, renew them, rely on them, then relay the truth on to your children. It will hold you fast through the turmoil of your future.[3]

From these accounts it can be seen how the experience-based wisdom of grandparents and great-grandparents has impacted and is impacting grandchildren. Jay Kesler, chancellor of Taylor University in Upland, Indiana, in writing about this, pointed out that grandparents can serve as a spiritual catalyst to the younger generation, demonstrating for them the reality of life in Christ.

The grandchildren of all of these grandparents saw that demonstrated in their day, and it followed them throughout their lives and is now impacting the lives of their children and grandchildren.

To observe growing children move into adolescence and on into young adulthood and then marry and establish homes of their own, where they have had the loving example of grandparents whose faith was lived out daily, shows the progression of faith taking root and growing in grandchildren who choose to follow in the footsteps of their grandparents. It is true that people who have a heritage of godly grandparents carry this influence in their lives forever. Sometimes they don't even realize it.

I've read and studied Christian books on the market now on this subject of grandparenting, and in all of them I see a passionate plea for Christian grandparents to stand in the gap in our culture, doing what God requested in Ezekiel 22:30.

At the outset of writing this chapter, I prayed and opened my Bible and immediately opened to Ezekiel 22. My eyes went to verse 30, which speaks of the prophet looking in vain for anyone who would build the wall of righteousness to guard the land, for someone to stand in the gap and defend against enemy attacks. That is the need which exists today, as much as, if not more than, in the days of Ezekiel. Today that gap is widening. There are not enough grandparents passing on familial faith. There are not enough grandchildren who have received the faith of their fathers into their own hearts and lives.

Directly after finding that verse, I found an article in my file by Dr. Kesler in which he talked about this. God has a way of getting our attention, doesn't He? God did find a man to stand in the gap. He sent His own Son to do for His children what they could not do for themselves. Jesus stood in the gap for us. Let us make certain our children and grandchildren know they can trust the man who died for them. By our words and by our lives, may we be found faithful.

The anthem "Find Us Faithful" speaks to my heart. It has a message for us, as grandparents, and for our children, grandchildren, and great-grandchildren.

> As those who've gone before us,
> let us leave to those behind us
> the heritage of faithfulness passed on thru godly lives.
> O may all who come behind us find us faithful
> may the fire of our devotion light their way.
> May the footprints that we leave
> lead them to believe
> and the lives we live inspire them to obey.
> After all our hopes and dreams have come and gone,
> and our children sift thru all we've left behind,
> may the clues that they discover
> and the memories they uncover
> become the light that leads them to the road we each
> must find.[4]

"Those who have been given a trust must prove faithful" (1 Corinthians 4:2).

ADDENDUM:

A WORLD GONE WRONG

Listen to me, you who know righteousness,
You people in whose heart is My law:
Do not fear the reproach of men,
Nor be afraid of their insults....
My righteousness will be forever,
And my salvation from generation to generation.
—ISAIAH 51:7, 8b (NKJV)

In the aftermath of the 9/11 attacks, Christian organizations were to be found at "ground zero," at the site of the World Trade Center. The response of the American people was united as we stood shoulder-to-shoulder, inspired by the bravery of our nation's firefighters, police officers, emergency workers, and the many civilians whose names we will never know. Despite unspeakable losses, this tragedy united us. As Billy Graham said, "Difficult as it may be, this event can give a message of hope—hope for the present and hope for the future."

That is the message we must continue to transmit to our grandchildren. No doubt, hundreds of thousands of children were asking questions like Martha Ashworth's 11-year-old grandson asked: "Grandma, is this the end of the world like in that big battle the Bible talks about?" This wise grandmother seized the opportunity to reinforce the truths of the Bible, reassuring her grandchild of God's love and telling him that God is in control of all events. Nothing takes Him by surprise.

EVERYBODY CALLED HER GRAMMY

My grandson Dustin sent me a story of a grandmother who was on one of the planes that crashed into the World Trade Center. Her grandson attends the same college he does:

> Everybody called her "Grammy," but her name was Thelma Cuccinello, and she was 71.
>
> Hanging on the quilt rack in her home in Wilmont, New Hampshire, are pieces of cloth waiting for Grammy to assemble. It is labeled "Emily" and slated for the youngest of Cuccinello's 10 grandchildren. Completed personalized covers wait for her other grandchildren, the names proof of a grandmother's love: Patrick, Shane, Keith, Bryan, Caroline.
>
> "She'd put them away in different places of the house," her daughter, Cheryl O'Brien, recalled Wednesday, a day after her mother's flight slammed into the north tower of the World Trade Center. "She was saving them for when they were older."
>
> Her care extended to Albert, her husband of more than 50 years and O'Brien's father. "There are meals now in the freezer for my dad, labeled for each day for the week she'd be gone," O'Brien said.

Cuccinello was on her way to visit her 75-year-old
sister in California. "They'd lived on opposite sides of
the country for much of their lives but alternated visiting one another," O'Brien said.

Tuesday it was Grammy's turn to make the trip.

"She wanted to spend more time with her sister
because she was getting older and wasn't sure how
much more time they would have," O'Brien said.

Cuccinello had lived in Lexington, Massachusetts,
most of her life before moving to Wilmot 10 years ago.
Still, she often returned to Lexington, usually squeezing
in a visit to nearby Bedford, where her daughter and
grandchildren lived.

"If my kids cut their fingers, she was there," O'Brien
said.

O'Brien's proximity to Logan International Airport
was another plus. Whenever she traveled, Cuccinello
would arrive at her daughter's home the day before the
flight, spending a night with her brood before heading
skyward. Monday was no different.

Nor was Tuesday morning. Daughter took mother
to the bus before daylight. She had a confirmed seat
on American Airline flight No. 11, scheduled to lift
off from Boston at 7:59 A.M. Destination: Los
Angeles.

"I was the last one to see her," O'Brien said.
"I got to kiss her and say 'I love you' and 'have a nice
trip.' "[1]

Dustin phoned several times following the events of September 11th, and we talked about Grammy. He wrote an e-mail in which he said that we, as Christians, don't have to fear:

> What is it that people fear the most? Why do they fear? "If God is for us, who can be against us?"... The Lord God Almighty who controls the heavens and the earth is more powerful than we could ever imagine. God is giving us opportunities to respond to what happens around us. Instead of trying to avoid the difficult things that happen, we need to look to God for guidance in the way He would have us handle things.
>
> There will be situations throughout life that will be very difficult to understand. Just because we are Christians doesn't mean we are protected from this world. Bad things happen because this world is full of sin. This is a world gone wrong. We will go through valley-of-the-shadow-of-death times, but God picks us up and carries us through....

Dustin wrote from the experience of going through the cancer trauma. His brief essay showed that he was thinking and responding thoughtfully and biblically. I was pleased and thankful for his reasoning and this demonstration of his faith and trust.

Grammy's story gives us pause for reflection. Are you doing all you can to prepare your grandchildren to make the final trip? Do your grandchildren know that they can be safe forever in God's heavenly home?

How would you rate yourself as a Lois?

APPENDIX:
THE READING WAY TO GROW

In visiting with a young mother, she expressed concern about the many forces and influences competing for the time and attention of children. She said, "I feel inundated by societal pressures that I don't want to pass on to my children."

We talked about what grandparents can do to help parents. One of the things that came out of that conversation was her recognition that what goes into the impressionable minds and hearts of young children is going to lodge there and influence them greatly. "Not all our friends understand the importance of nurturing the thought life of their children," she said.

I was happy about that conversation for it underscored what I have long known and felt strongly. I have always emphasized that a person is himself plus the food he eats, the friends he makes, and the books he reads. Philippians 4:8 clearly sets forth the need to guard our thought life. In 1 Timothy 4:8, the apostle Paul told Timothy to take the time and trouble to keep himself spiritually fit. Paul exhorted Timothy to "give attention to reading." His emphasis was on reading the Scriptures. "Meditate on these things; give yourself entirely to them, that your progress may be evident to all" (v. 15, NKJV). And in his last letter to Timothy, Paul asked him to "bring...my scrolls, especially the parchments" (2 Timothy 4:13). Could Timothy ever forget the example of his mentor? Never!

It Takes Time to Keep Spiritually Fit

When I was in the Christian bookstore business, I heard many excuses as to why people don't read. They boiled down to three main reasons:

• "I don't have time." People ask me, "How do you find the time to read?" One doesn't *find* the time; one *takes* the time. If you are too busy to read and keep spiritually fit, you are, indeed, too busy! People always make time for the things they really want to do.

• Books cost too much. There was a time when a man could get a haircut for 25 cents. Can you imagine it! Or gas—some of us remember what we used to pay for a gallon of gas—certainly not what we pay today! And what about clothing? We haven't given up haircuts, driving cars, or keeping up with the latest styles. Is our vanity such that we are willing to spend what it takes on our outward selves but unwilling to spend anything on that which will enrich our personalities and nurture the inner man?

• I'm not a reader. Any habit worth developing is worth working at. Reading is a habit that takes time to cultivate if you aren't a natural-born book lover. Children with their curiosity and eagerness to learn and explore can easily be nurtured on to the reading habit. As grandparents, we can help to grow readers in our grandchildren. Did you learn to play golf in your first round? How about sewing: did you learn overnight? Consistent doing develops habits that result in skills and expertise.

Substandard reading material, or little or no reading, is bound to result in substandard thinking and living. We want the best for our grandchildren; let's work at this business of helping to motivate them to become readers. Many years ago, I heard Dr. Howard Hendricks say that one of the most crucial means of stretching your mind is through the process of reading. The mind is like a muscle. It develops with use. You won't wear it out. No one ever dies with a brain that has been totally used. That will never happen. Though you do need to constantly stretch your mind, be careful what you feed it, because what you feed it will largely determine what you are.

Eyes have been opened, hearts melted and life-changing decisions made through the pages of books. I recall asking a man if he had read a certain book. His answer? "Yes, I read it, and I felt it, too!" Such feelings are bound to produce action that has its effect not only in the life of the one responding to what he read, but in the lives of others around him as well.

Henry David Thoreau said, "A truly great book teaches me better than to read it. I must soon lay it down and commence living on its hint. What I began by reading, I must finish by act-ing." Certainly the best book is not one that merely informs, but one that stirs the reader to do something with what he has read.

A great philosopher once said, "My mind is myself. To take care of myself is to take care of my mind."

If another beatitude were to be added to those that Jesus gave, I think I'd suggest: "Blessed be the lovers of books and those who feel the need to read." And I'd say, "Blessed be those parents and grandparents who help to nourish the minds of their children and grandchildren through reading."

In her book *The Hiding Place,* Corrie ten Boom recorded the words of the old rabbi who said to her father, "Books do not age as you and I do. They will speak still when we are gone, to generations we will never see. Yes, the books must survive." Mention the name Corrie ten Boom and her many books, and you will find an appreciative audience. But the old rabbi had it right—books can be our spiritual mentors, especially those by authors like A. W. Tozer, Andrew Murray, Hannah Whitall Smith, and Brother Lawrence, just to mention a few saints and writers of a generation past. Our great-grandparents would have "given their eyeteeth" (as the old saying goes) to get their hands on the books we have at our disposal today. Books by Dr. James Dobson, Dr. Charles Swindoll, Max Lucado, Dr. Howard Hendricks, Barbara Johnson, Florence Littauer, Stuart and Jill Briscoe, Gary Smalley and John Trent, J. B. Phillips, C. S. Lewis, and the list could get very long.

When it comes to children's books, a walk through our local Christian bookstores reveals so much to choose from it's easy to feel overwhelmed. Take the time to ask your bookstore staff for recommendations. Introduce your grandchildren to the world of Christian books by letting them accompany you.

An old proverb says, "Wear the old coat; buy the good book."

Consider what reading does for you: Reading equips you to be a thinking Christian—exactly what Paul told Grandmother Lois's grandson he was to be!

MASTER THE BIBLE—AND LET IT MASTER YOU

Standing apart from all other books is the Bible. Read God's Word first. The new translations and paraphrases can help. And remember what John Locke said, "Reading furnishes our mind only with materials of knowledge. It is thinking that makes what we read ours."

Dr. A. W. Tozer asked:

Why, after years of Christian profession, do so many persons find themselves no further along than when they first believed?...The reading habits of the average evangelical Christian in the U.S. are so wretchedly bad as actually to arrest his spiritual development and block the progress of the faith he professes to hold.

Personal accountability for pursuing excellence in our lives is what it's all about. We all need a deeper acquaintance with the God of the Bible, His Son, Jesus, and with the work of the Holy Spirit. We need that which will help us in our relationships and in life experiences. And we need this throughout our lives. To help our grandchildren acquire a love of reading is to help them grow.

BIOGRAPHIES

Biographies will challenge the impressionable minds of your grandchildren to achieve greatness. Eric Wiggin's fine book *The Gift of Grandparenting* (Tyndale House / Focus on the Family, 2001) lists some biographies for grandkids. Right on, Grandpa

Eric! Kids love reading about heroes and heroines. We can counteract our secular culture with biographies of Christians.

Some of the most thrilling reading both you and your grandchildren will ever enjoy can be found in the *Heroes of the Faith* series published by Barbour Publishing. You can find these books in Christian bookstores. Billy Graham, Jim Elliot (one of the five fellows martyred in Ecuador in 1956), Eric Liddell (Olympic medal winner), C. S. Lewis, Martin Luther, Mother Teresa, William and Catherine Booth (founders of the Salvation Army), and Jonathan Edwards (the Great Awakener) are just a few of the personalities covered. If you don't have access to a bookstore, you can order them from Barbour Publishing, Inc., P.O. Box 719, Uhrichsville, OH 44683, or call 1-800-852-8010.

Youth With a Mission (YWAM) also publishes a series of mostly missionary biographies. If you don't find these in bookstores, you can call 1-800-922-2143, or write: YWAM, P.O. Box 621057, Orlando, FL 32862-1057.

Mott Media publishes *The Sower* series, with 26 titles and growing. To order, call 1-248-685-8773, or check with your bookstore.

Bethany House publishes the *Men and Women of Faith* series, including more than two dozen books (1-800-328-6109). But check with your Christian bookseller first. Such bookstores are Main Street missionaries who can introduce you to all kinds of wonderful books and videos for your grandchildren.

You might also want to enroll your grandchildren in God's World Book Club by phoning 1-800-951-2665 and asking them to send information.

MAGAZINES AND PERIODICALS

Focus on the Family publishes *Clubhouse Jr.* (ages 4–8), *Clubhouse* (8–12), *Brio* (teen girls), *Breakaway* (teen guys), and *Brio & Beyond* (older teen girls). *Plugged In* (for both teens and parents) offers reviews and commentary on the latest music, movies, and television programming aimed at youth. *Boundless* is a Webzine for college-age young adults, designed to engage their hearts and minds; it's free and they will love it (www.boundless.org). To request these resources, subscribe, or just to learn more, call 1-800-A-FAMILY (232-6459) or log on to www.family.org.

NOTES

Chapter Four: A Profound Influence

1. Alexandra Stoddard, *Mothers: A Celebration* (New York: William Morrow, 1996), p. 220.
2. Ibid.
3. Edith Schaeffer, *What Is a Family?* (Grand Rapids, Mich.: Revell, 1975), p. 132.

Chapter Five: A Powerful Force

1. Dale Evans Rogers with Carole C. Carlson, *Grandparents Can* (Grand Rapids, Mich.: Revell, 1983), p. 12.
2. Dale Evans Rogers, *The Woman at the Well* (Old Tappan, N.J.: Revell, 1970), p. 25.
3. Ibid., p. 19.
4. Ibid., pp. 19–20.
5. Ibid., p. 22.

Chapter Six: A Grandfather of Faith

1. To find out more about Linda's and Danny's ministry to the disabled, contact: LUVability Ministries to the Disabled, P.O. Box 46, Niles, Michigan 49120 Ph: (616) 687-5054 Web site: www.luvability.org E-mail: lability@skyenet.net

Chapter Seven: That Gifted Way

1. *The South Bend (Ind.) Tribune*, August 26, 1990, *Opinion* section.

Chapter Eight: Intercessors: The Righteous Faithful

1. Received from T. W. Wilson's widow, printed with permission of Byron Bledsoe.

Chapter Nine: The Silent Saviors

1. Evelyn Christenson, *What Happens When We Pray for Our Families* (Colorado Springs, Colo.: Victor, 1992), p. 20.
2. The exact source of these comments is unknown. Ask for Kesler's books at your Christian bookstore.
3. To find out more about Elaine Shelton's "Off Our Rockers" group, contact her at P.O. Box 17516, West Palm Beach, FL 33416 Ph: (561) 683-0226 Web site: www.sonic.net/thom/oor/ E-mail: OffOurRockers@worldnet.att.net
4. "The Fine Art of Grandparenting," AARP *Bulletin,* July–August 2000, p. 13.
5. Ibid., p. 2. You can write to AARP's Grandparent Information Center at 601 E. St., NW, Washington, D.C. 20049, or go to www.aarp.org/bulletin.
6. "Who Should Decide Whether Grandparents Can Visit?" *USA Weekend,* January 7–9, 2000, p. 16.
7. Christenson, *What Happens When We Pray,* pp. 12–13.
8. Dr. Joyce Brothers, "Terrible Family Secrets," *Parade,* August 14, 1994, p. 17.

Chapter Eleven: The Crowns of Grandparents

1. Helpful Web pages for tracking lineage: Ancestry (www.ancestry.com), Genealogy Gateway (www.gengateway.com) and GenForum (genforum.genealogy.com).

2. Tom Dodge, "Grandpa: A Link to Older Era," *Dallas Morning News,* November 12, 2000, p. 2F.

Chapter Twelve: A Grandparent's Essence

1. Charlotte Moss, *A Passion for Detail* (New York: Doubleday, 1991), p. 19.

Chapter Fourteen: Grandchildren and Death

1. Joe Bayly, *The Last Thing We Talk About: Help and Hope for Those Who Grieve,* rev. ed. (Elgin, Ill.: David C. Cook, 1992), p. 25.

2. Many passages in the Bible provide this assurance, including Luke 9:23-25; 17:33; 2 Corinthians 5:6-9; and Philippians 1:21; 3:7-12.

3. Martin R. De Haan II, "The Legacy," *Discovery Digest* 112.

4. Excerpted from the "In Memoriam" booklet presented at the memorial service of Dr. V. Raymond Edman.

5. Bayly, *The Last Thing,* p. 7.

6. Ibid., p. 64.

7. C. S. Lewis, *A Grief Observed* (New York: Bantam Books, 1961), p. 69.

8. Bayly, *The Last Thing,* p. 106.

9. Joseph M. Stowell III, "When Trouble Hits, Go with What You Know," *Discovery Digest* 110.

10. For more information on the Indigenous People's Technology and Education Center (I-TEC) or on Steve Saint, go to www.I-TECusa.org. Or write: I-TEC, Steve Saint, 10575 SW 147th Circle, Dunnellon, FL 34432. I-TEC is a charitable organization. Steve's book *The Great Omission* is also available.

Chapter Fifteen: Responding to Crises

1. Dr. James Dobson, *When God Doesn't Make Sense* (Wheaton, Ill.: Tyndale House, 1993), p. 121.

2. Dobson, *When God Doesn't Make Sense,* p. 231.

Chapter Sixteen: A Grandparenting Potpourri

1. Vicki Bohe-Thackwell, *Too Skinny to Float* (San Jose, Calif.: Writers Club Press, 2000).

2. As told to Evelyn Hinds, August 23, 2001. Used with permission.

Chapter Eighteen: Experience-Based Wisdom

1. Charles R. Swindoll, *You and Your Child* (Nashville: Thomas Nelson, 1977), p. 160.

2. Charles R. Swindoll, *Rise and Shine,* (Portland, Oreg.: Multnomah, 1989), pp. 159, 160–161, 163.

3. Ibid., pp. 162–163.

4. John Mohr, © 1987, Birdwing Music/Jonathan Mark Music (admin. by Birdwing Music/ASCAP).

Addendum: A World Gone Wrong

1. Christy Oglesby, "A Grandmother's trip ends suddenly, awfully," CNN.com © 2001. All rights reserved.

Welcome to the Family!

Heritage
Builders®

Helping You Build a Family of Faith

We hope you've enjoyed this book. Heritage Builders was founded in 1995 by three fathers with a passion for the next generation. As a ministry of Focus on the Family, Heritage Builders strives to equip, train, and motivate parents to become intentional about building a strong spiritual heritage.

It's quite a challenge for busy parents to find ways to build a spiritual foundation for their families—especially in a way they enjoy and understand. Through activities and participation, children can learn biblical truth in ways they can understand, enjoy—and *remember.*

Passing along a heritage of Christian faith to your family is a parent's highest calling. Heritage Builders' goal is to encourage and empower you in this great mission with practical resources and inspiring ideas that really work—and help your children develop a lasting love for God.

* * *

How To Reach Us

For more information, visit our Heritage Builders Web site! Log on to **www.heritagebuilders.com** to discover new resources, sample activities and ideas to help you pass on a spiritual heritage. To request any of these resources, simply call Focus on the Family at 1-800-A-FAMILY (1-800-232-6459) or in Canada, call 1-800-661-9800. Or send your request to Focus on the Family, Colorado Springs, CO 80995. In Canada, write Focus on the Family, P.O. Box 9800, Stn. Terminal, Vancouver, B.C. V6B 4G3

To learn more about Focus on the Family or to find out if there is an associate office in your country, please visit www.family.org

We'd love to hear from you!

Other Faith and Family Inspiration
From Focus on the Family ®

The Gift of Grandparenting

Grandparents are one of the most important influences in the lives of their grandchildren. *The Gift of Grandparenting* shows grandparents how to take an active role in creating strong spiritual and emotional ties through activities emphasizing fun and faith. Whether the grandchildren live around the corner or around the country, this book gives every grandparent new ways to enjoy the marvelous gift of grandparenting.

Heart to Heart Stories for Grandparents

Grandparent and grandchild . . . was there ever a closer bond? It plants roots, history and a wise love no one else can share. Celebrate memories of grandfather and grandmother as you enjoy Joe Wheeler's collection of favorite stories that bridge the generation gap and bring us all back home.

LifeWise

This bimonthly magazine enriches lives of those in mid-life and beyond with articles on health, finances, marriage, service and family communications—plus inspirational stories, humor and book reviews.

Add Life to Your Years

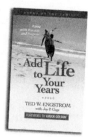

This remarkable book paints dozens of portraits of seniors who are aging with passion and purpose. Ted Engstrom's interviews will amaze and inspire you and challenge your notion of "retirement."

Focus Over Fifty Web Site
Timely features that inspire, encourage and inform.
www.family.org/focusoverfifty

•　•　•

Look for these special resources in your Christian bookstore or request a copy by calling 1-800-A-FAMILY (1-800-232-6459). Friends in Canada may write Focus on the Family, P.O. Box 9800, Stn. Terminal, Vancouver, B.C. V6B 4G3 or call 1-800-661-9800.

Visit our Web site (www.family.org) to learn more about the ministry or find out if there is a Focus on the Family office in your country.